BROOMCORN NOSTALGIA:
Field Of Memories

Includes real life experiences in the old days (mostly 20's and 30's) when broomcorn flourished in America. The author and Burl Ives grew up in broomcorn country.

A good example of the past that needs to be preserved for future generations.

Alice Babbs Smith

Olde Mill Publishing
Santa Barbara, California

Copyright ©1996 by Alice Babbs Smith

All rights reserved. No part of this book may be reproduced or transmitted in any form or by any means, without written permission from the publisher.

Broomcorn Nostalgia: Field of Memories
by Alice Babbs Smith

Olde Mill Publishing
Post Office Box 6342
Santa Barbara, California 93160

ISBN 0-9655768-0-9

Library of Congress Catalog Card Number 97-91538

Printed and bound in the United States of America

First Edition

12345678910

Cover: Artworks, Instructional Development, University of California Santa Barbara

Cover Photo: A field of broomcorn in Illinois by Mark Jones, Arthur, Illinois

ORDER FORM on last page

IN MEMORY

Memories that mother gave to us are beautiful and rare—her selflessness, her love of life, her smile, a sense of humor to ease her cares and help others to see that living is worthwhile.

These are treasure we give to our own, and they in turn will give to theirs.

The love she gave us will never end, the things she taught us we teach again. In our lives her life repeats and death retreats, inane before the power of this endless chain.

Minnie Phillips Babbs

CONTENTS

ACKNOWLEDGEMENTS	i
LIST OF ILLUSTRATIONS	iii
AUTHOR'S NOTE	v
PROLOGUE	1
PART ONE	11

    A Palace in the Middle of Main Street
    What in the World is Broomcorn?
    An Unprecedented Festival
    Let's Attend the Festival
    The Amish at the Festival
    Amish Remedies for Various Health
        Problems

PART TWO	49

    A Closer Look at the Plant Without
        Ears
    Early History—Broomcorn and
        Brooms
    Benjamin Franklin Introduces
        Broomcorn to America

> The Niskayuna Shakers
> Early Inventions Have Competition
> Broomcorn Capital in Early Days

PART THREE   73

> Days of Horsedrawn Buggies, Kerosene Lamps and Pot-bellied Stoves
> What Else Went on While Broomcorn Flourished?

PART FOUR   109

> Down on the Farm During Broomcorn Days

PART FIVE   129

> Benjamin Franklin "Returns" and Asks Questions

PART SIX   155

> Why are Brooms Called by that Name?
> A Blind Broommaker
> The Amana Colonies
> Making a Broom With Ancient Machinery
> Let's Make a Broom at a Factory
> Do Brooms Have Standards?

PART SEVEN   177
    Brooms and Superstitions
    Poem: Aunty's Broomcorn Broom
    Sweep That Weight Away!
    Don't Stand Me on My Straw End!
    Recipe: Broomstick Cake

CONCLUSION   187

GLOSSARY   193

RESOURCES   195

CREDIT FOR ILLUSTRATIONS   197

ACKNOWLEDGEMENTS

I wish to thank the following for making it possible for me to complete this book:

Arcola Chamber of Commerce, Arcola, IL; *Arcola Record-Herald*, Arcola, IL; *Associated Press* (Theresa Humphrey); *The Miami Herald* (Dave Barry); *Champaign-Urbana News Gazette*; Earl Clark, Arcola, IL; John and Mary File, Champaign, IL; *The Gazette Company* Cedar Rapids, IA; Handy Andy Broom Company, Lindsay, OK; Lydia Hemrich, Effingham, IL; Ted Hocking, Mt. Carmel, IL; Burl Ives, Anacortes, WA; Michelle Jaeger, Fresno, CA; Gertrud Lawson, San Diego, CA; P. A. Lindenmeyer, Arcola, IL; Lindsay Oklahoma Chamber of Commerce; Mission Country, Goleta, CA; The Thomas Monahan Company, Arcola, IL; National Broom Company, Stockton, CA; Newton Broom Company (Anna Rohr and Becky Shamhart), Newton, IL; Oklahoma State University (Professor E. E. Weibel); *The Early History Of Arcola* (Cynthia Rothrock); *Santa Barbara News Press*; Madelyn (Maggie) Stapp, Santa Barbara, CA; Texas Agricultural Experiment Station; Elizabeth R. Turner, Oakland, CA; University of Illinois Agronomy Department (Dr. H. H. Hadley); Don and Marie Ward, Newton, IL; Warren Bros. Broom

Field of Memories

Co. (Louis Turner), Arcola, IL ; Ye Olde Broom & Basket Shop, West Amana, IA.

Special thanks to the author of *Eric Sloane's America* (Eric Sloane), published by Galahad Books, NY, for information about Pioneer America. His book shows us how to appreciate the past. Finally, I will be eternally grateful to granddaughter Heather Simioni for all her help in bringing this dream to reality.

LIST OF ILLUSTRATIONS

AUTHOR'S NOTE
Map of Illinois

PROLOGUE
Burl Ives

PART ONE
Broomcorn Palace of 1898
Sketch of Buggy, Similar to Amish Vehicle
At Festival: Sweeping Contest
Road Race
Dave Barry, Humorist, *The Miami Herald*
The Arcola Lawn Rangers
Winner, Antique Auto Show, Larry Black
Arcola Band's Broom Corps Leading the Band
    Through the Parade
Marching Band
Floats:
    "Amazing Arcola"
    The Rockome Garden
Winding Brooms at Festival in Broomcorn
    Tent
Parade (Various Photos, Including Antique
    Vehicles)

PART TWO
Benjamin Franklin
Raggedy Ann and Andy

PART THREE
Model T Ford
Clara Bow Hats

Field of Memories

PART FOUR
Field of Broomcorn, Oklahoma

PART FIVE
Broomcorn Knife
Curing Shed for Broomcorn
Tabling Broomcorn
Cutting from the Table

PART SIX
Ye Olde Broom & Basket Shop, West Amana, Iowa
Making a Broom with Ancient Machinery (Series of Photos)

PART SEVEN
Witch Riding a Broom

AUTHOR'S NOTE

Before completing *Broomcorn Nostalgia*, I was very saddened to hear of the death of my friend, Burl Ives. He had encouraged me to write about broomcorn and the olden days. He too, grew up in the Midwest, Hunt City, Illinois, near my hometown of Newton. We attended the Newton Community High School. Our roots are imbedded in broomcorn country.

Burl, a natural entertainer, had a special love for children and young people. His recordings of folk and children's songs included "The Blue Tail Fly," (chorus Jimmy Crack Corn) and, among his albums, "The Best of Burl's for Boys and Girls." Upon his return visits to Illinois from California, Burl would sometimes play his guitar and sing for young people. Afterwards he would encourage them to get an education. "Never quit school!" he would say.

People in Santa Barbara, California, remember Burl Ives as a great celebrity who assisted worthy causes by generously giving his time and talent. In 1986 he was Grand Marshal of Old Spanish Days Fiesta Parade. Riding in a horse-drawn carriage he and his wife, Dorothy, and a grandchild headed the procession.

The theme of my book is to preserve a way of life many people have come to cherish. Carl Sandberg wrote in his book

Field of Memories

Harvest Poems 1910-1960 (Cornhuskers 1918, Prairie): "The land and the people hold memories . . . they keep old things that never grow old." Burl Ives was a part of those memories, a part that will never grow old.

Burl's wish to be buried next to his parents' graves in Mound Cemetery, east of Hunt City, Illinois, (his birthplace) was fulfilled. Here his ashes are interred. Here a huge granite monument at the gravesite bears the etching that is just below his picture holding his guitar:

> One of Americas legendary entertainers whose career spanned more than a half century crossing all international borders. Equally at home before the royalty of Europe and the farm folk of Midwestern USA. A performer whose unique style adapted to all media. Literary. Radio. Movies. Recordings. Night clubs. Broadway and Concert Stage. Carl Sandburg called him "The mightiest ballad singer of this or any other century."
>
> June 14, 1909   April 14, 1995

Burl's widow, Dorothy, said that Burl spoke daily of his roots in Illinois, of Hunt City, Newton, Jasper County, for almost 30 years.

Mother, your children's upbringing—our roots—never left us. Burl, also born in broomcorn country, by his life gave the world an example of how a family should be. Lessons taught him never left him.

Field of Memories

Just as Burl Ives' ballads will live on to inspire coming generations, broomcorn nostalgia will also live on and on.

Broomcorn Nostalgia

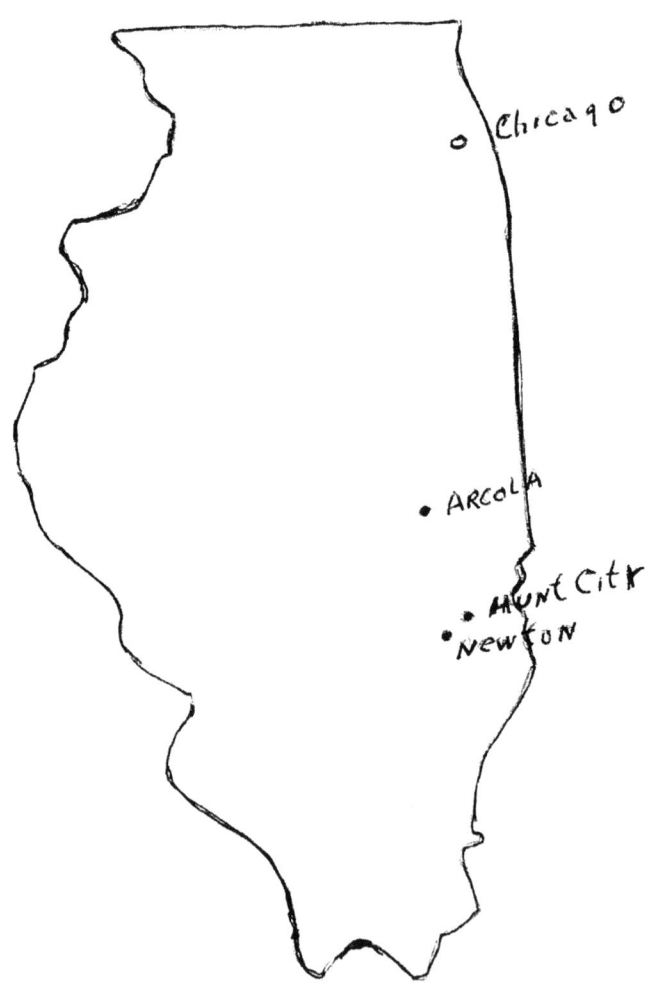

Arcola: Site of Broomcorn Festival
Hunt City: Burl Ives' Birthplace
Newton: Author's Birthplace

PROLOGUE

*"Oh, the broomcorn plants,
they have no ears,
they have no ears —
and that's not all;
their heads are cut off
and made into brooms
at harvest time in the fall."*

My mother's voice, small with age, trailed off. Though barely five feet in height, she sat tall in her chair that September morning. A widow in her nineties, she lived alone in Newton, a small Midwestern town in Illinois. Vigorous of mind, with a keen sense of humor, her family roots were deeply imbedded in the soil of the farmlands.

With a twinkle in her eyes, she asked, "Do you think I could be competition for Burl Ives?"

"Well, Mom," I said, "Burl once defined a folk singer as 'one who relates to the country, the soil . . .'"

"I know. And I think Burl's father raised corn near here a long time ago . . . let's see . . . about the time women in America won the right to vote."

Like Burl Ives, my mother believed "everything comes from the land and, eventually, everything dies and goes back to the land." Farming, to her, was a way of life—in communion with the land. Relating to the land was something she did all her life.

"The earth is eternal," she said. "People come and go but land lasts forever."

Even in her eighties, while living in town after my father's death, and despite ill health, mother tended a big garden, including long rows of corn.

"Work is the key to progress," she once said, "and using the brains God gave you. Idleness is a tool of the devil."

Frowning, she continued, "Too many young people are idle. Give 'em work to do and a gathering place to have good, clean fun. Let 'em work hard and play hard."

Hard work and hardships did not dim mother's love of the farm.

"The great Depression was a frightening time," she said, "but we had it better than many. Our farm provided us with food, but we had to work hard."

Mother's energy and enthusiasm appeared to have no bounds, but there came a time, after several bouts with illness, when her doctor said, "No more gardening, Mrs. Babbs. Your daughter is to take away all your garden tools."

Did this stop my mother? No, indeed. That's when she started a mini-garden a few feet from her back door. She had no garden tools, no hose to use in watering. My sister found her, however, in all her glory, "hoeing" her vegetables with a big butcher knife. Using water from her kitchen faucet, she filled a pail and watered her plants.

Reluctantly, she allowed someone else to tend her garden, but she kept tabs on it from her kitchen window. She always gave generously of her share of the garden produce: sweet corn, potatoes, green beans, onions, tomatoes—whatever was ready to use.

A questing mind led her to read a great deal. Even when her eyesight became dim and glasses could not help she kept up on world events.

"It's hard to believe anyone could go to the moon," she said. "Seemed like a miracle when I watched on TV. I wish your grandparents could have known about it."

Born in Illinois of sturdy stock, the only girl in a farm family with six brothers, she told how she loved to dress in overalls and tag along with her brothers to help in the fields. She admitted to being a tomboy in those days.

My parent's farm, near Newton, was only a few miles from Hunt City, Burl Ives' birthplace. At that time the area was broomcorn country.

Minnie Phillips Babbs helped to raise and harvest many acres of broomcorn, but she had never been to the Broomcorn Festival—a big event held in the fall in Arcola, Illinois, a distance of about forty miles. When she sang about the broomcorn plants she looked forward to attending the festival.

The following morning, however, my mother did not come out singing. She smoothed her white hair that had been neatly combed straight back, but curled softly around her face—an ageless face. The day before she had her hair cut and waved in anticipation of attending the festival, but now, as she hobbled out to the kitchen, I knew her arthritis was "acting up."

I could see disappointment in her eyes as she said, "Wish I could go, but my legs . . . Maybe next year." She brushed away a tear.

To see the longing in her eyes brought moisture to my own, and I wished that

California were closer to Illinois so that I could visit more often.

Something in the set of her head suggested pride undaunted by pain when she picked up a sturdy cane and with a grimace, slowly moved her arthritic legs across the room to a window facing the street.

"See that factory across the street? That's the Newton Broom Company. I remember when Burl Ives visited there with other students from our high school. They make thousands of brooms at the factory every month, and every year someone from their office brings me a nice broom. Didn't you visit Burl's sister-in-law, Opal, here in Newton?"

"Yes. Opal said that Burl left Charleston College (Illinois) later called Eastern Illinois University, with his guitar. Seems he knew he had to do his own thing. Later, he attended the famous Juilliard School of Music in New York. He composes, you know."

Mother nodded. "And he studied in cornfields. He lived on a farm, a houseboat, and in a mansion."

"Yes," I said. "He certainly wasn't one to put on airs. His 'Jimmy Crack Corn' style of music is really popular, so full of oomph. And he sings with such ease."

Mother sighed. "Wish I could be that relaxed. Now he lives so far away—doesn't get to Newton very often—but it's great to have him come. You know, the helicopter he arrives in lands on the high school football field."

"I know. And he liked football. He was fullback on the Newton High School squad. Mom, even in high school, students sensed that one day Burl would be a famous person. We enjoyed his guitar playing, his singing, his sense of humor."

Mother said, "People here in Newton were happy when he became successful. You know he claims an audience of all ages."

"Yes, Mom, and not only by his songs, but on radio, the stage, movies, and TV acting. And wasn't he born near here?"

"Yes. Just east of Hunt City, I believe in June, 1909. I surely liked his radio show, *The Wayfaring Stranger*."

I asked, "Didn't Burl travel quite a lot?"

"Indeed he did," mother replied. "He loved Ireland and its people."

"We're part Irish, aren't we, Mom?"

Mother laughed. "Isn't everybody? Well, not quite everyone . . ."

"Oh, yes, Burl liked to go sailing," she added. "He once said, 'It's nature and you alone, and you feel pretty unimportant, and that's good for you.'"

"He's really humble," mother continued. "Never needed a mansion to live in nor a trip abroad to be happy, though I remember (I believe it was in '78, late August) when he stopped here in Newton on one of his visits. He'd been abroad on a tour, three weeks of concerts in Israel. He and his wife, Dorothy, had tea at Golda Meir's home. He sang in London and Norway during his trip. Oh, before going on the tour he had just finished filming the TV movie, *Heidi.* Remember? He played the part of grandfather."

"Yes . . . in a press release from Eastern Illinois University, Burl Ives was quoted as having said the following about the Midwest: 'I think the fact that I'm from Illinois has a lot to do with what I'm about. Even beyond music, the Midwest always was a very substantial part of who I am. I was born in the country, brought up with cornbread and milk and greens. That makes a big difference—gives you stamina.'"

Tongue in cheek, I asked mother, "Did you know that Burl Ives has been compared to Benjamin Franklin?"

"How?"

"In a book on the life of Franklin, I believe by S. G. Fisher, it is written: 'He never said a word too soon, nor a word too late, nor a word too much.'"

Mother laughed. "Oh-oh! Ya got me."

For many years my mother had been kidded by family about being such a big talker.

Now, grinning, she changed the subject. "About broomcorn," she began, "Burl Ives has seen it growing in fields in this area. Your father and I used to haul many a wagon load to the broom factory here. Now it's trucked in from Mexico. Doesn't pay the farmers to raise it."

She leaned forward in her chair, eyes bright with excitement. "I just thought of something about the festival. You can tell me about it, of course, (after you go) but, better yet, why not write about it, and all about broomcorn and brooms. And write down some of the things that happened in the olden days while broomcorn flourished. I bet some people have never even **heard** of broomcorn."

"You're right, Mom. And I couldn't find any books on it at the Santa Barbara library."

Mother is now dead. She lived to be 95, many years after my father's death. It was a terrible blow when he died, but it didn't extinguish her indomitable spirit. A strong-willed person with a big heart who danced when she was happy is now still. She left a legacy of courage to her family. Her sense of hope and of joy made a lasting impression upon all eight of her children. "Laugh and the world laughs with you," she would say.

Her long life, characterized by exuberance and a sense of humor, reminds me of a Proverb: "A joyful mind maketh age flourishing: a sorrowful spirit drieth up the bones."

At mother's request, and in her memory, I have written about attending a famous Broomcorn Festival and, with the help of others, I hope I have written "all about broomcorn and brooms, and some of the things that happened in the olden days while broomcorn flourished."

Burl Ives

Broomcorn Nostalgia

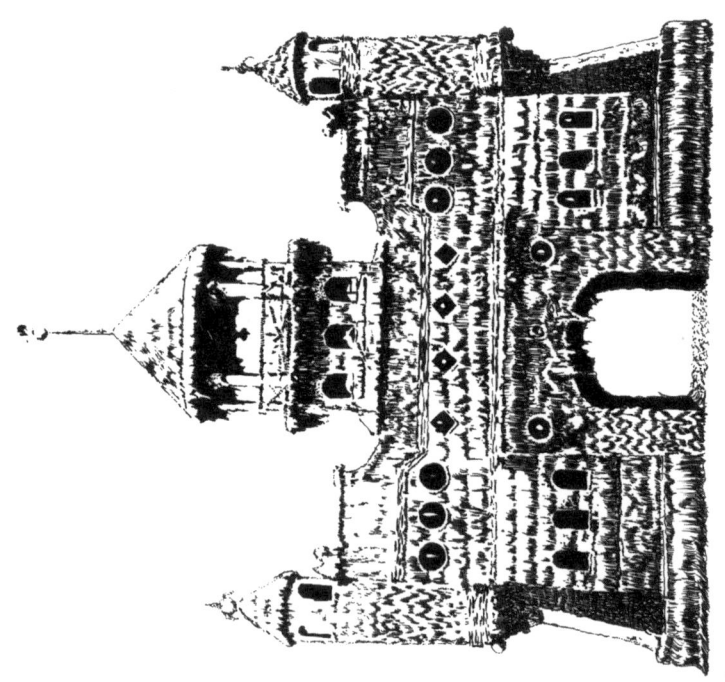

Broomcorn Palace of 1898. Reproduction by Gertrud Lawson, San Diego, California

Field of Memories

> *Nostalgia is like a*
> *grammar lesson;*
> *it makes the present*
> *tense and the past*
> *perfect. (anonymous)*

PART ONE

A palace in the middle of Main Street. An "empty palace where friendly ghosts of the past linger." Picture this palace, four stories high, constructed in the middle of Main Street in the late 1800's. The palace reaches across the street. Horse-drawn vehicles pass through the opening in the lower level of the palace.

The street is crowded with people of all ages who have come to attend a celebration. All eyes turn toward the newly completed palace—a most unusual structure—completely covered and thatched with **broomcorn**. This was the year of the famous Broomcorn Festival and Street Fair in Arcola, Illinois, a small Midwestern town about 150 miles south of Chicago.

What in the world is broomcorn? You got a hint when you read the Prologue. It is not the kind about which Burl Ives sang in "Jimmy Crack Corn." The plant has no ears, and the brush-like head (the tassel) referred to as "brush" is the valuable part. Because the straws are long and flexible and very strong the broomcorn crop is used in the manufacture of brooms and brushes. It belongs to the sorghum family. Broomcorn resembles Indian corn in appearance and habit of growth. A complete description is included in PART TWO, but now, more about the Festival.

Since 1971, annual broomcorn festivals have been held every fall in Arcola. It's one of the most unusual events in the nation, an unprecedented and refreshing festivity. It's a renewal of the first broomcorn festival in America, more than a century ago. It celebrates the area's broomcorn heritage, recalling the days when Arcola was known as the Broomcorn Capital of the World.

In attending this festival, just as my mother wished, I experienced a need to preserve a way of life many people have come to cherish. Although none has ever duplicated the original broomcorn palace it is traditional to have a palace at each festival, for when broomcorn no longer grows in the various areas of America where it once flourished, there's a yearning as for something lost.

Have you ever had a desire to retreat into the past when things were more peaceful, to get away from the stress of everyday living? Evocative of pioneer America, the festival bears out what novelist Mary Wallace wrote: ". . . it's a powerful thing—the hold the past has upon us. What has been is never really lost. It's the foundation upon which our teetering modern world rests, and we have a deep need to be reminded of it."

To those who love the soil the festival offers satisfaction. It makes sure that the era which has gone before will not have been in vain. The festival proves that people's relationship with Nature—with the soil—is enduring.

Arcola is in the center of a farming community. On either side of the highway as you approach Arcola, the rich, black soil is carpeted with endless acres of Indian corn. It stands tall, a symbol of prosperous farmlands. There is something solid in a field of growing corn.

PEOPLE COME

At the festival they love to partake of all that the original Broomcorn Palace of 1898 represents. Not only from all over Illinois do visitors come. License plates indicate they are from many other states as well. They arrive by auto, truck, bus, train, bicycle, motorcycle, camper, large motor home, on foot, and the Amish by horse-drawn buggy. Families who like to focus on a simpler days' atmosphere, to recall an era that was serene, are drawn here. It appears that residents of small towns are better able to preserve a way of life Americans hold dear.

Let's join the crowd at the festival. It consists of people of all ages. Warm temperatures draw a shorts and T-shirt crowd, especially among the younger people. Older visitors experience a nip of nostalgia. Kiddies have fun, and many young people (some not so young) take part in the activities.

We now enter the festival grounds. There's free parking. No admission charge. As we move ahead there's much to engage the senses. Freshly popped corn and hot dogs bring instant hunger to kiddies, as well as to adults. Cinnamon rolls, spicy apple butter simmering, apple fritters, grandma's cinnamon delight, and fresh cider whet the appetite. You may be tempted to try the pancakes and sausage. In late afternoon, chicken and fish dinners are served.

Local church groups serve food in their basements, or on the lawn during the festival. You can count on homemade delicacies being served each day.

Every year the festival has new attractions. The Chamber of Commerce sponsors the event—with a lot of hard work

Field of Memories

by hundreds of people in Arcola —both before and after the celebration.

    The festival is held downtown, with the parade along Main Street. Arcola is an authentic one-mainstreet town. During the weekend of the festival it's amazing how many people attend. Although the population of Arcola in 1980 was only 3,000, at festival time this number greatly increases. In 1979, 26,000 attended, with the largest number showing up at parade time. On Saturday, at the festival of 1981, a crowd of 42,000 attended. In 1982, 52,000 were present for the three-day event, which started at 3:30 p.m. on Friday. And would you believe in 1992 the attendance swelled, pushing a total of 70,000 for the three days. The Chamber of Commerce was happy with the large crowds in 1993, 1994, and 1995. Headlines in the *Arcola Record-Herald* September 14, 1995 indicated the Broomcorn Festival "Biggest and Best Ever." Large crowds are anticipated in years to come.

    Signs on store windows on Main Street indicate they are closed because of the festival. Shops vie for attention, however, with their window displays, and the sidewalks are splashed with store sale items.

    If you have a sweet tooth you'll admire the display of jams, jellies, and preserves. This brought to mind the heavy shelves in my parents' basement where, every year, similar jars stood—along with fruits, vegetables, and meats. All were grown on the farm and processed by my mother on a stove fueled by wood from trees cut down by my father on our land.

Your senses will be caught up by the sounds of music. Each year a variety of entertainers sing and play musical instruments. I thought of Burl Ives, remembering the first time I heard him, accompanied by his guitar, sing "Jimmy Crack Corn." Old-time music, religious and popular songs, entertains. You may hear Blue Grass music—a down home pickin' and singin' style of country music. To further spice the program, there might be a jazz band, a barber shop chorus, and a kitchen band. All this draws enthusiastic audiences.

There's a Beer Tent, and a German band. Inside the Beer Tent a delicious Brautwurst dinner is served.

For children's entertainment, past festivals have included a kiddie carnival, a mini-tractor pull, a mini-farm exhibit with farm animals children can see and touch, and of course plenty of food and soft drinks. Strolling magicians have provided entertainment, as well as an organ grinder accompanied by a cute little monkey that kept busy accepting coins from youthful visitors.

GAMES AND CONTESTS

All contests carry prizes or notoriety. Ever count the number of straws in an ordinary household broom? At the 1976 festival a prize was given to the person who came closest to guessing the correct number. Just to watch people examine the broom proved interesting. One youngster had a calculator, but others kept pushing him away. A gentleman from St. Louis guessed 1,714, which was closest. The correct number was 1,709 straws.

Want to enter a National Sweeping contest? It's a preview to the festival proper. Entrants use a broom (a corn broom) to see who can sweep the most broomcorn seeds through a maze in a given amount of time. It's a contest of speed and skill, with the winner eligible for entry in the Guinness Book of World Records if able to break the previous record.

Have you ever played Broom Ball? It's a game resembling hockey, except the implement used to propel the ball is a corn broom. Despite a few sore muscles for some players it's lots of fun.

In a game called "Curling," brooms have a major role. Ice or artificial ice is required. Four players on each team slide a forty-pound stone made of granite, with a handle on it, at a circle target at the corner end of the court. When the heavy stone is released and slides down the ice, the stone

Field of Memories

Sweeping Contest, *News Gazette*, Champaign, IL, R.K. O'Daniell, September 7, 1980.

is so constructed that it has a natural tendency to curve or "curl." To lessen the curl and direct the stone to an intended target, a specially made broomcorn broom is used by a player to sweep rapidly in front of the stone as it slides down the ice.

A log sawing contest involves skill, strength, and teamwork. Two men are pitted against two opponents on a cross cut saw.

Festivals have included other contests: hollering—featuring the national champion, a tug-of-war team, pie eating, cake decorating, little Miss and Mr. Arcola contest, climbing a greased pole, raw egg pitching, and digging for dollars—a hunt in mud for silver dollars.

DEMONSTRATIONS

Everyone, both young and old, seem to enjoy watching demonstrations of old-time crafts at the festival. These have included cornmeal grinding, sorghum making, cider pressing, apple butter making, blacksmithing, shingle making, chair caneing, duck carving (no, not live ducks), and the operation of a steam engine—the kind used for threshing more than a half century ago.

At the 1976 festival an old-fashioned grist corn mill was on display. In 1979 there were Civil war exhibitions and a battle skirmish with a bunch of "Confederates." A lot of gunpowder went up in smoke before the Confederates were subdued. Even Abe Lincoln was portrayed—looked just like his picture—sponsored by the First National Bank of Arcola. The long rifle demonstrations in 1980 interested many, but to a three-year-old lass it was too much noise and she became frightened. She was soon comforted by her parents, however.

A SPECIAL EVENTS FEATURE

One of the Big Ten's greatest all time cross-country runners, Craig Virgin, appeared in the annual ABC 10,000 meter road race at the festival two years in a row. Virgin had previously set a new American record for the 10,000 meter race with a time of 27.394 during the AAU National championship in Walnut, California. Participants in this race have fun.

About 260 runners completed the annual 5,000 and 10,000 meter races at the 1992 festival. Anyone twelve years of age or older is eligible to enter.

Young folks have enjoyed the Teen Dance on Saturday evening. The Pre-1950 Antique Auto Show is popular, as well as "Broomcorn Harvesting," and a "People Pull." In 1989 members of the Star Pulling Team pulled and tugged a 4,000-pound sled 155 feet in two attempts to take their seventh straight championship.

The theme for the 1975 festival was "Sounds and Sights of Yesteryear." The

The Road Race, Arcola Record-Herald.

festival committee attempted to recreate the rambunctious noisy atmosphere of hundreds of broomcorn "johnnies" or "canaries." For years these migrant workers helped farmers harvest and process broomcorn. In the early 1900's, during harvest time, Arcola was filled with these harvest hands. Because of the workers' unannounced arrival—like birds in spring—they were called canaries. Their wages were paid in accordance with the number that arrived. The more workers there were the quicker the harvest was finished, and this resulted in fewer hours for each worker.

QUILT DISPLAY

Many old-fashioned items are on display at the festival, but one caught many eyes—the quilt display. Beautiful and colorful, the quilts were made in assorted patterns by women in the Arcola area. Countless hours of tedious work, no doubt, were spent in making these bed covers like grandmothers or great-grandmothers used to make. Quilting parties were a common occurrence in those days, with neighbors gathering together to visit and work at the same time.

ARTS AND CRAFTS

A large display of arts and crafts exhibited by local talent drew considerable interest in 1980. Displays for sale ranged from tole painting and oil painting (with demonstrations of each) to artificial floral exhibits.

THE PARADE

Who doesn't love a parade? Thrill to the sound of bands marching down the street, perhaps a dozen or more, and a drum and bugle corps. Though each year brings new attractions to the three-day festival, you can regularly see a mile-long parade on Main Street, as well as flea market stands, the Broomcorn Tent, and a replica of the Broomcorn Palace of 1898.

The parade brings a feeling of exhilaration. Children excitedly call out, "Look, Mom, Dad, there's Jim . . . and Carol!" (or whoever is in the parade). Cameras click. On view are exhibits that reveal in part what life and times were like when broomcorn was king in the area, e.g., antique autos, trucks, and tractors. Antique farm implements parade the streets together with modern ones, so you will see classic vehicles, horse and pony drawn units, and horse and rider. Not to go unnoticed are beautifully decorated floats, clowns, and happy youngsters on bicycles.

Small courtesies may be seen among those present to view the parade. One very warm day I saw a youngster about three years of age offer a piece of ice from her drink to a perspiring, elderly man seated near who was fanning himself with a small hand fan. Another youngster offered his folding chair to a woman who was standing.

SPECIAL ENTRIES

Each year brings special entries, for example, a 20-horse hitch. The Old Gold Seed Company had **20 horses in front of the wagon.** In 1982 Country Western singing star, Cal Smith, who made "Country Bumpkin" song of the year and record of the year in 1974, entertained with two shows. The same year, Victor the "Rassling" Canadian bear, was another attraction. Weighing 550 pounds and 7 feet, 6 inches tall, he took on all challengers and won. Of course his canine teeth and claws were removed. According to his trainer, Victor knows eighteen different wrestling holds. Keeping in front of the bear at all times was necessary in order not to be squashed if he should sit down on you. Garth Brooks, entertainer at the 1990 festival, drew record crowds.

Over the years, has there been much change in programs at the festival? Let's take a look at the newspaper, *Arcola Record-Herald*, which contained the following ad on September 10, 1992, page 12:

> "Come to our renewal of the original
> Broom Corn Festival and Free Street Fair
> Established in 1898 – Re-established

annually starting 1971
Friday – Saturday – Sunday
September 11, 12, 13, 1992
Beginning September 11 at 12 noon
On our Main Street in
ARCOLA, ILL.
Arts and Crafts
Huge Flea Market
A huge old fashioned parade
at 3 p.m. Saturday, Sept. 12.
ABC 5,000 and 10,000 Meter Races
Broom making
Broom Factory Tours
Arts and Crafts
Homemade Goods
Miller Beer Tent with Entertainment
Sweeping Contest
Contests and other Entertainment
Talent Show
Teen Dance
Pre-1950 Antique Auto Show
Broom Corn Harvesting
People Pull
Old Fashioned Demonstrations
Flea Market
HOMEMADE DELICACIES SERVED ALL THREE DAYS
Van Dells Sept. 12, 1992
1 p.m. & 6 p.m. at Oak St. Stage
Tracy Lawrence Sept. 13, 1992
1 p.m. & 3 p.m. at Oak St. Stage"

Near the Main Street festival area there was a convenient plot of land that contained broomcorn ready for harvest. There, harvesting demonstrations by longtime residents were provided. Mother would have loved to reminisce and see that demonstration showing just how it was done "in the olden days."

Tracy Lawrence enhanced the reputation for top quality entertainment with two shows Sunday afternoon.

The Van Dells, an Ohio based rock band (1950's and '60's), gained popularity with their music, dancing, and comedy.

Why was the attendance in 1992, pushing the 70,000 mark for the three days, a big increase over previous years?

Besides being one of the most unusual festivities in the nation, a combination of perfect weather, the festival's growing reputation for top quality activities and entertainment, and the featuring of Pulitzer prize winning syndicated humor columnist Dave Barry at an Arcola high school assembly, all contributed to its success. Major television, radio, and newspaper reporters covered this feature on Friday, September 11.

Dave Barry returned for a second straight year to the festival, accompanied by a Miami camera crew. The crew filmed various festival events for a special television program, "Visions of America," syndicated by Group W of Westinghouse, and was broadcast in November, 1992.

Barry, along with several other celebrities, was invited to present his vision of America. A 1991 Arcola Lawn Ranger,

Broomcorn Nostalgia

Dave Barry, Humorist, *The Miami Herald*

Barry chose the famous Arcola Broomcorn Festival for its fun but small town atmosphere. When he spoke before a student assembly at Arcola High School, both students and faculty alike enjoyed the humor of his tongue-in-cheek tales.

Looking at members of the Arcola football squad, he said, "You're going to (win) tonight. I can tell by your haircuts." Arcola **did** win—53 to 0. Players gave Barry a Purple Riders T-shirt after his speech.

Barry attended most of the 1992 major broomcorn festival events, ran in the 10-kilometer race, and danced to King and the Jukebox Jammers in the beer tent before leaving Sunday morning.

He spoke of trying to improve his Lawn Ranger form in the parade from the previous year. However, Pat Monahan, squad leader for the Lawn Rangers, had to agree with Barry that he had all the grace of a corpse.

Prior to the 1993 festival parade, Arcola residents peered at cloudy skies. **Don't rain on our Parade!**

Their requests were granted. Saturday, September 11th, thousands lined the streets to see the record 201 parade entries. The Governor of Illinois, Jim Edgar, and Secretary of State, George Ryan, marched in the parade.

It did rain Sunday morning, the 12th, and festival Chairman, Randy Rothrock, became concerned. The rain stopped,

The Arcola Lawn Rangers, *Rankin Publishing*

however, and scheduled events, though delayed, did take place.

A huge crowd gathered to hear country singer, John Michael Montgomery, perform. A popular young singer, he delighted the crowd with vibrant versions of country songs from his album in the making—*Life's a Dance*.

According to Mike Lindenmeyer, food stand chairman, 1993 "would have been a record year without question, had it not been for the rain." Even so, attendance was estimated to be about 60,000 for the three-day festival.

Pat Monahan, beer tent co-chairman, indicated "there was plenty of opportunity to be entertained, fed, and to shop—all at a reasonable price."

The Vogues drew a crowd with their blend of classic 50's music, country and western favorites and on-stage antics.

Dave Barry returned for the 1993 broomcorn festival and participated in the 10-kilometer race. He again marched with Arcola's world-famous Lawn Rangers, a top precision lawn mower drill team. He wrote in one of his humor columns published in newspapers including the *Santa Barbara News Press* November 1, 1993: "We also carry brooms and we perform precision broom-and-lawn-mower maneuvers, such as the extremely difficult (for us anyway) 'Cross and Toss.'" He tells of marching with a 10-foot-high painted concrete statue of Elvis.

"It's mounted on a trailer, facing backward, and it weighs 5,000 pounds ... the Rangers, more than 50 strong, stride in two columns down the parade route, pushing our mowers in front of us, raising our brooms on high at the command 'Brooms Up!'; meanwhile, bringing up the rear, glinting in the Midwestern sun is: Elvis' giant concrete butt."

After Barry returned to his room at the Arcola Inn where Elvis' statue also stayed, Barry remarked, "I can see him on his trailer in the parking lot, looking into the distance, as if waiting for somebody to deliver a giant concrete pizza .... Things are good here in the Midwest. Weird, but good."

Neal McCoy's popularity as entertainer at the 1994 festival rivaled that of Garth Brooks who entertained at the 1990 festival. McCoy's singing and dancing energized festival goers. In his first show crowds sang along with familiar numbers including "King of the Road," "Rockin' Robin," "Doo Wah Ditty Ditty," and with his hits "Wink," and "No Doubt About It." Original country hits, pop classics and the standard "Danny Boy" were creatively mixed.

For his second show he added his songs "Mudslide" and "Small Up, Simple Down," Elvis Presley's "Teddy Bear" and The Temptations' "My Girl." McCoy and all members of his band wore official Arcola Broomcorn Festival T-shirts for this show.

According to Arcola Chamber of Commerce President Kim Van Gundy, "It was the largest crowd we have had for an entertainer." People literally lined the rooftops around the Oak Street Stage.

As always the parade was a big part of the festival. The Arcola band's "Broom Corps" led the band through the parade.

In the Float category the Rockome Gardens float took first place. The Antique Auto show was won by Larry Black of Decatur, with a 1966 Mustang.

Part of the scheduled entertainment at the Beer Tent had to be canceled. In its place Gary Kinder and Steele Wheels played both country and rock classics for large crowds.

Like others in the past, the 1994 broomcorn festival was a huge success.

FLEA MARKET

People browse with abandon at the flea market stands covering three blocks at the festival. The large display of antique items open glorious doors to the past. Hundreds of nostalgic items are displayed on long tables, from antimacassars to water well pumps. Workers from broomcorn fields washed up for dinner (served at noon) with water from hand pumps such as these.

An item that brought a bit of melancholy was an old tintype of a large family, unidentified. Surely it was a duplicate of a cherished photo. It lay beside

Winner, Antique Auto Show, Larry Black with a '66 Mustang, *Arcola Record-Herold*, 1994.

Field of Memories

Arcola Band's Broom Corp, '94 Parade, Arcola Record-Herald.

Marching Band, '92 Festival, *Arcola Record Herald.*

Field of Memories

Float "Amazing Arcola," *Rankin Publishing*

The Rockome Garden Float, 1994, *Rankin Publishing*

some picture post cards of yesteryear with sentimental messages for Valentine's Day.

BROOMCORN TENT

Come in to the broomcorn tent. Here individual broommakers display their crafts and you can watch them ply their trade. The Thomas Monahan Company of Arcola sets up exhibits of locally made brooms in the tent.

If you wish to purchase a broom there's a great variety from which to choose: household brooms, hearth, hand-made, toy, janitor, warehouse, and whisk brooms. PART SIX has complete information on making brooms, together with photos.

Just outside the tent are healthy-looking stalks of freshly cut broomcorn, tall and green, brought in from fields in the area.

THE THOMAS MONAHAN COMPANY

Represented at the festival, the Thomas Monahan Company is one of the world's largest brokerage firms, universally famous. It introduced broomcorn processing in Mexico, where it obtains most of its broomcorn supply. This company sells its product extensively in Central and South America, in Canada, and to a lesser extent in the Orient, as well as in the United States.

Winding brooms at festival in broomcorn tent, *Arcola Record-Herald*.

For more than a century the Monahan Company has been associated with brooms and broomcorn. Patrick H. Monahan became the first broomcorn broker in Illinois in 1869, and he paved the way to making Arcola the Broomcorn Capital of the World. The Monahan firm buys the broomcorn, stores it in its warehouse, then sells it to the broom manufacturer. As a broomcorn dealer or brokerage firm, the company also keeps on hand all the necessary items to make brooms.

Features of the festival have included a tour of the Thomas Monahan Company, and also a tour of the Warren Bros. broom factory in Arcola, as well as to a broomcorn field.

At the 1992 festival the Monahan Company assembled a float, "Amazing Arcola." Banners on the float indicate several of the outstanding activities Arcola is noted for, including Raggedy Ann Festival, Arcola Broomcorn Festival, School Spirit, and Tourism.

In addition to the Warren Bros. broom factory, another broom factory in Arcola, the Libman Broom Company, established in Chicago in 1896, claims to be the largest broom manufacturer in the world. Their brooms are marketed throughout the United States. Other broom factories are mentioned in PART SIX.

THE AMISH

Amish families living in the Arcola area who attend the festival drive there in horse-drawn vehicles, usually buggies. Their religious beliefs require that they shun modern technology.

A gentle people who dress simply and neatly, the Amish are descendants of a strictly religious sect that split from the Mennonites in the 17th century. Their homes are clean, the grounds well kept. They take good care of animals, and use draft horses to pull their plows. They have no modern machinery.

They don't concern themselves much about the outside world. Most are farmers. They believe in following as closely as possible the ways of the past, dressing as their ancestors did and maintaining their homes without decoration. There are no phones, radios, or television sets. Believing that cars destroy family life, they own no cars. Nothing is sold on Sunday.

Well versed in the soil, they raise good crops. Women help with the harvest. The elderly are treated with great respect. No one is ever placed in an old people's home. Amish men must grow beards when they marry. The lives of the Amish are serene, and they appear happy in their slow-paced lifestyle. They don't believe in education past the eighth grade. Basically, they have their own schools, and a ruling that their children can leave school after age 14.

The Amish teach children to work, and to enjoy work as rewarding and fulfilling. They believe in the Bible and use it as a family guide. They don't believe that electricity and modern world things are necessities.

At the festival one year I sat near a young Amish mother. She was keeping an eye on two little girls about four and six years, who were laughing and jumping about during the parade. They looked cute in their bonnets and long white dresses. Their pink, shining faces appeared to have just been scrubbed. The mother, about 25 years old, wore neither jewelry nor cosmetics. Her light blue cotton dress was long, and a matching bonnet covered her head. She was an attractive woman, and when she smiled at the children her eyes filled with pride.

After the parade the three disappeared into the crowd, but later I saw them, together with the father, who was wearing a large black, widebrimmed hat. While driving away from the festival in a horse-drawn buggy they returned my smile, and the children waved.

The Amish use simple remedies for their ills. For colds and coughs, they use honey and lemon, onion plaster poultice and poho oil. For injury, they use aloe vera, vinegar, onion salve and Vitamin E. For stomach ailments, they believe comfrey tea and aloe vera juice are helpful. For circulatory problems, they turn to white oak bark, calcium tablet and myrrh.

The Amish people show respect for the past. Most young people do. Future generations can be influenced, molded by happenings and people in the past. Those who have lived in Arcola, Illinois, and in surrounding areas for many years pass down to their children and their children's children memories of an era that will live on and on.

Field of Memories

Broomcorn Nostalgia

Field of Memories

"There is nothing new under the sun."

PART TWO

We have attended the Broomcorn Festival as my mother wished, and now we will go forward to learn "all about broomcorn and brooms, and life in the olden days while broomcorn flourished."

How can broomcorn resemble Indian corn, yet produce no ears? When I was a child this puzzled me the first time I saw it growing in my father's fields in the fall. **How strange**, I remember thinking, **no ears**. We have already learned that broomcorn belongs to the sorghum family. There are saccharine (sweet sorghums) and non-saccharin sorghums. Perhaps you have eaten cookies or gingerbread made with sorghum.

Broomcorn is the oldest variety of the nonsaccharine sorghums which include: Kaffir corn, milo maize, durra (doura, dhourra or dhoura), and Jerusalem corn, as well as broomcorn. The seed heads of broomcorn, when compared to Indian corn, have longer, straighter straws which form the brush of the plant. These seed heads are usually brown and oval. They are inside bristly bracts that are reddish, tan, or mahogany colored. The stalk of the plant grows up to 15 feet tall, depending on the variety.

When I asked one of my grandsons in California if he had ever heard of broomcorn, he replied, "I think it's something that was grown in the United States in the olden days." He was correct, except that it's presently produced in many countries, though over the years, in smaller quantities.

WHERE GROWN

Broomcorn is grown in Mexico, as well as the European countries of France, Hungary, Italy, Greece, Yugoslavia and Romania. Australia and the South American countries of Argentina, Brazil and Uruguay produce crops of it, as well as Chile and Peru. Some Asian and African countries grow it as an experiment.

Broomcorn was king in Illinois until after World War II when it started dying out due to the scarcity of migratory labor to harvest the crop. From then on it was produced in the United States in Oklahoma,

Colorado, New Mexico, and Texas. Now discontinued in these states, it is practically all grown in Mexico. Virtually all the broomcorn now grown in Illinois, which is a small amount, is grown for seed.

The green broomcorn stalks outside the festival tent kindled memories of my father's cornfields. How beautiful the crops looked during good years, green fields growing tall in the summer sun.

Thomas Jefferson believed that "those who labor in the earth are the chosen people of God," and that "the farmer is the most noble and independent man in society."

In those days farming was a way of life. Besides working hard, farmers were self-reliant and had values that may be dying out elsewhere in our country.

Early one Saturday morning in July, I accompanied my father to the cornfields. A warm earthy smell rose from the ground.

Dad bent down near a stalk, listened for a moment, then whispered, "Hear it growing?"

"You have to be joking."

"No, listen!"

With my ear close to the stalk I did hear a soft, rustling sound. There was no breeze at the time. That day I knew that happiness to my father was hearing the corn grow.

Like Robert Green Ingersoll, my parents believed that "in Nature there are neither rewards nor punishments. There are consequences." They loved to farm, to commune with nature, and that love was passed on to all eight of their children. Nature, the eternal teacher, voiced meaning in their lives and bestowed hope.

Growers of broomcorn in early days also loved to commune with nature. Let's go back to those days.

EARLY HISTORY OF BROOMCORN AND BROOMS

In this country, a published volume titled *History of Hadley, Massachusetts* by Sylvester Judd, first mentioned broomcorn. The town of Hadley was settled in 1659, and Mr. Judd states in his book: "Broomcorn, the sorghum saccharatum of botanists, a native of India, has long been cultivated in the southern part of Europe, chiefly for seed, but brooms and brushes were made of it in Italy, more than a century since." The broomcorn plant itself was first described in Italy in the 16th century.

How did people in ancient and medieval times keep their homes clean? About the 13th century the Chinese developed a broom **Kaoliang** with long fibers.

Early natives used an article fashioned by tying twigs or fibers to the end of a stick when they wanted to clean out some trash. Another cleaning device was made by splitting a four-foot long hickory stick from the end to within a few inches of the other end, then wetting and bending these small splinters down and tying them into a bundle. Round in shape, the bundle varied in size, as did the shape of its handle.

BENJAMIN FRANKLIN

There might never have been a broomcorn festival had it not been for Benjamin Franklin. He has been called "The Father of the American Broom Industry." He has the honor of being the first to introduce broomcorn to the United States. The year was 1725.

We know that Mr. Franklin was a famous person, one of the great heroes of our history: a signer of the Declaration of Independence and the Constitution of the United States, a diplomat, statesman, author, inventor, and a shrewd business man. He was responsible for many "firsts." One was the hiring of a street cleaner. In 1757, Mr. Franklin's report to the Philadelphia Assembly concerning the service resulted in the passage of a bill for the service. His publication *Poor Richard's Almanac* was filled with useful information and advice. He spent many years of his life teaching thrift and common sense to his fellow Americans before he died in 1790.

Mother and Benjamin Franklin had something in common. Both were thrifty.

Benjamin Franklin

They believed in "waste not, want not." Neither could stand to see anything that might be of use wasted.

Mother knew that balls of string came in handy, and seeds from healthy garden plants saved the cost of purchasing seed packets. Coffee grounds, eggshells, and vegetable peelings helped garden soil to become more productive without purchasing fertilizer.

While Mr. Franklin was cleaning dust from his hat with a whisk broom, he became curious when he saw seeds attached to the fibers of the broom. No doubt, he didn't want to ignore what possibly could be something of use, so he removed a seed and planted it in his Philadelphia garden. (Accounts differ as to his whereabouts when he obtained the seed and the source of the whisk broom.)

The resulting plant appeared to have little value, but became a garden novelty and, for a few years, was only an ornament in several Philadelphia gardens. At the time, no one was aware that one day a part of similar plants would be made into a great cleaning tool. Had there been television in those days, the plant would possibly have been identified because it was grown in other countries.

Later, in New England, it was discovered that by tying some of the fiber from the plant to a stick a cleaning tool could be made.

Early American production of broomcorn centered in two areas, New England and Virginia.

In 1781, nine years before Benjamin Franklin died, Thomas Jefferson placed broomcorn among the main agricultural crops of Virginia. That state, however, was not the first to produce it commercially. This credit was given to Massachusetts.

A bachelor named Levi Dickinson who lived in North Hadley, Massachusetts, obtained a handful of the seeds, took them home, and in the Spring of 1796 planted them. That fall he had enough straw to make thirty brooms. Since the small crop turned out well, he planted a half acre the next year and made several brooms. The following year (1798) he planted an acre which produced enough straw to make between 100 and 200 brooms. He could now afford a wife, but he chose to remain a bachelor.

What a tedious task it must have been for Mr. Dickinson (lonely, too) to make his own broom handles and spin his own twine. For awhile, a man named Heber helped him tie on broom until Mr. Dickinson worked out a better way. He wound string around a roll which he placed under his feet, and, while sitting in a chair, he wound the string around the brush in his lap. Using a knife, he scraped the seed from the brush, and later used the edge of a hoe with a short handle, fastened to a bench. Finally, it was discovered that upright teeth improved the procedure.

How did Mr. Dickinson distribute his brooms?

For those he made in Massachusetts, he used a horse-drawn cart to peddle them. He sold brooms in Williamsburg, Ashfield, and Conway. The people in his home town of Hadley considered him dreamy-minded, impractical, and some taunted him with snide remarks. Dickinson, however, did not allow anything to divert him from his course—even his ill health. He boldly predicted, as early as 1801, that the broom industry would be the greatest in the country.

When Mr. Dickinson began to prosper from his venture, his former critics went into the broomcorn business. By 1810 more than 70,000 brooms were made in the Hadley area, and in 1843 the business was firmly established in America. That year Mr. Dickinson died at the age of 88.

Even in the early days, when selling slowed down, occasional "tricks" were used. The story is told about one of the star salesmen who had a load of brooms for sale down in the state of "wooden nutmegs" and "brass hams." At the time he found trade rather dull. Going into a store, the man named Lombard (nickname Old Lumbud) made his usual opening, "Any brooms today, sir?"

"No, not today," the merchant replied.

"Better buy some, sir," Lombard urged, and continued, "Store trade, sir."

That looked good to the merchant so he said, "All right, bring them in."

Upon hearing this, Old Lumbud said to the man with him, "You take in half and I'll take in half."

The merchant, after paying for half the brooms in money, said, "Now what will you have in store trade?"

Old Lumbud replied, "Take brooms, sir, take brooms." And he carried out **the half that the merchant had paid for!**

NISKAYUNA SHAKERS

If you've wondered who was the first to fashion brooms in their present shape, the answer is: a religious colony called the Niskayuna Shakers. About 1834 they began to raise broomcorn in the Mohawk Valley of New York. Many growers of broomcorn had moved westward into the Mohawk Valley because they discovered broomcorn in that area grew better brush. The Shaker broom which was introduced looked like the present broom in shape. They had spread the fiber and sewed the broom so it would cover more sweeping surface. Rougher corn was put on the inside, more of it put on two sides of the handle opposite each other, and the result was then flattened by a press to hold it in shape. This added to the broom's streamlined appearance. Soon sales began to increase.

Credit was given the Shakers for designing the first winder and sewing vises, thus enabling a broommaker to make many times the number of brooms he could tie by hand.

An old Shaker Journal published at Boston, Massachusetts contains the following entries:

> Harvard, Mass., Jan. 9, 1843: "Some of the brethern are a-chopping timber and wood at the south pasture woods. They worked there two or three days last week. Elijah Myrick works at the saw mill sawing boards. Augustus at the blacksmiths to get iron works done for a shingle machine and broom press."
>
> Feb. 23, 1843: "Thomas Holden and Alfred Collier sled wood and logs from the south pasture lot. Brother Joseph Mayo and Dana White work at sizing broom brush. Augustus works at the mill."
>
> March 24, 1843: "Augustus at the mill making broom handles."
>
> Jan. 13, 1844: "Some rainy in the morning and some sloppy and splashy. Elijah Myrick makes a lot of broom handles."

The Mohawk Valley of New York finally stopped growing broomcorn, and production moved to Ohio, Tennesee, Pennsylvania, Wisconsin, Missouri, Indiana, and Illinois.

SEED BROUGHT TO ILLINOIS

In 1867 Mr. John Cofer, an Illinois farmer living near Arcola visited in

Tennessee where he became interested in the plant and its uses. He brought several bushels of broomcorn seed back to Illinois, and here he and his neighbors planted it. Broomcorn fields had now fingered their way into the fertile Illinois soil. There was a ready market for the brush at some of the factories just opened in Chicago.

BROOMCORN CAPITAL

Due to the soil and climate in Central Illinois, better quality brush was produced and corn acreage spread in Illinois, mainly to the south. Soon the Arcola area became known as the Broomcorn Capital of America, and, later, of the World. When broomcorn was "booming" in Illinois, the Central Illinois district was producing nearly half of all the broomcorn grown in the United States. About 1500 farmers in the Central Illinois district were growing this crop. Here was produced the best brush known.

Besides Illinois, other states began to raise broomcorn including Iowa, Nebraska, Kansas, and Oklahoma—the Lindsay, Oklahoma area in particular. Many settlers in that area, originally from Illinois, were experienced in caring for the crops. By 1936, 350,000 acres of broomcorn were grown in the United States.

BROOM FACTORIES

Though there were many early broom shops in New York, the first "real" broom factory was built in Amsterdam, Massachusetts, by G. W. J. Bronson. It was built before 1843, the year Levi Dickinson died. Soon other factories sprang up in the various areas where broomcorn was grown, including Virginia. Besides Virginia and Massachusetts, broomcorn was soon produced in other states, including Connecticut and New Jersey.

Early broommakers located near a source of supply of broomcorn because it was necessary to have all the help possible to cultivate and harvest the crop, the harvest beginning in September. By 1900 the largest manufacturers were centralized around the country, most of them near populous areas.

Since brooms were not easily available in rural areas, some farmers began to make their own. Others depended on a traveling broommaker who carried things necessary to make brooms: a knife, cords, a bundle of white oak splints, and a blunt needle with a large eye called a bodkin.

INVENTIONS

In 1875, Charles E. Lipe brought out the first sewing machine, and subsequently he and Alfonse Walrath combined their knowledge to make a Lipe and Walrath sewing machine.

A machine called a hurl cutter, which removed the brush from the corn stalk, was invented by Walrath. Then came sizing machines and power winders. Though inventors have improved the hurl cutter, tedious manual labor is still required.

BROOMS HAVE COMPETITION

Problems in the early broom industry caused by inventors came after World War I. The mechanical street sweeper replaced many brooms. The vacuum cleaner began to compete with the broom in the home.

In 1917, at the beginning of World WarI, supply shortages plagued the broom industry. However, in 1918 things changed for the better. A need for brooms overseas to help tidy up the camp areas resulted in shipments of brooms by the millions to France. In 1924 the Army discontinued the use of a curry comb and brush in favor of the vacuum cleaner to groom Army mules. It is said that some of the mules stubbornly refused to accept this new grooming device.

We have covered the early history of broomcorn and brooms, but what about Arcola, Illinois, in early days?

ARCOLA IN EARLY DAYS

Settlers came to the site now called Arcola in the mid-1800's. Pioneers decided to call this moist, open area covered by tall grasses the Grand Prairie. The first pioneers settled along riverbanks where there was timber, and later they moved to Grand Prairie.

Along the banks of the Kaskaskia River a small village grew. The river was called Kawkaw by the Indians (meaning Crow River), but because the settlers were unable to speak their language, they called it Okaw. Later, the village was named Bagdad. The Indians who formerly lived in the area had now gone, but when they were there they hunted prairie chickens, geese, ducks, deer, rabbit, and wild hogs on the Grand Prairie.

Businesses in Bagdad included a blacksmith shop, a brick yard, a mill, and a country store. Only a few items, however, could be obtained from the store: soup beans, coffee, or a keg of nails.

When news came that a railroad would be built that would cut through Grand Prairie there was much excitement. The railroad, one of the earliest to be built in the West, would join Chicago and the town of Centralia. A government grant gave the railroad some three million acres. With a lot of hard work, the railroad was finally finished and a new settlement formed along the railroad.

In the fall of 1855, a surveyor from Coles County laid out a piece of land on both sides of the railroad a half-mile wide. Knowing that the Illinois Central would cut through the middle, the settlers were pleased, and the first building in the new settlement was the Illinois Central Depot. Because of the nearby Okaw River, this settlement was named Okaw.

In the winter of 1856, villagers in Bagdad woke up to see snow and sleet that stayed on the ground for many weeks. Did they complain? No, indeed. Using nearby lumber as sleds, they skidded their buildings to the railroad and the town of Okaw. There was one exception: Daddy Grant, owner of the brick yard, refused to move—said he couldn't make bricks in a swamp. Okaw began to grow and, as the community spread out, with more settlers arriving and more homes and stores being constructed, there was a need for mail service. Soon people received mail twice a week by horseback. It was left at a place called Rural Retreat where Col. John Cofer was Postmaster. When the citizens decided it was time to have a post office, Col. Cofer sent a letter of request to Washington, D.C.

Washington reported that there was already a town named Okaw in Illinois, so a new name was needed. Folklore states that a Mr. James Kearney suggested the name "Arcola." Just how Kearney got his idea is unknown, but history shows that one of Napoleon's greatest battles happened at a bridge and place named Arcola in Italy.

As Arcola grew, new businesses were started, including a drug store, a dry goods store, a bakery, and a hotel. John Blackwell and his son, Samuel, started a lumber business. Then bad luck began. In May of 1858, a tornado destroyed many buildings in Arcola. A two-story hotel was not blown away, but a long pole from the railroad yards blew down through the roof and passed through the floor and into the ground. Some said that this pole was the only thing that kept the hotel upright.

Early schoolhouses were destroyed by fire, with arson believed to have been the cause of some. Lack of fire equipment caused Arcola to lose many buildings, the worst fire being in September, 1881, when more than twelve buildings were lost (including a landmark, the Illinois Central Depot). Despite the brave efforts of townspeople who formed a bucket brigade (using the water from nearby wells), they were unable to save the depot.

Efforts to form a high school in Arcola were in vain, and not until 1882 did anyone graduate from a high school there.

The first church in Arcola (Presbyterian) was built in 1860. Other churches were soon built: the Christian Church, St. John's Catholic, Methodist, Baptist, Lutheran, and an Episcopalian church.

Another railroad? This one ran East and West, passing through Paris, Arcola, and Decatur, and later connected to Terre Haute,

Indiana. A part of the Pennsylvania System, it was called the Illinois Midland, and in 1872 the first train passed over the line.

The following year the city of Arcola was incorporated. After an election was held and all votes were counted, there were 244 for, and only eleven against incorporating. After that many town elections were held, choosing people to run the city. Results of voting for buying fire-fighting equipment showed 137 against and only 63 for. Residents later sadly realized this equipment could have saved many buildings.

Who paved the way to Arcola becoming the Broomcorn Capital of the World? Patrick H. Monahan. He came from Ireland and started a business that brought growers and buyers of broomcorn together.

Major newspapers in 1903 carried the story of Arcola's coal raid. Because of coal strikes at the mines, Arcola was nearly out of coal to heat residents' homes. What to do? When a train loaded with the precious fuel stopped in Arcola for repairs, "Mayor Monahan and Policeman Craft ordered the coal cars off to the side."

As soon as the people of Arcola found out, they rushed with wagons, buggies, wheelbarrows—even bushel baskets—to pick up the coal. No, they didn't steal it. Every bushel was accounted for and within a week it was all paid for.

The next year (1904) Arcola residents took pride in the dedication of a new library. Whose idea was this? Tom Monahan, grandfather of Thomas Monahan, Jr., and Frank Collins, secretly worked on the library project. When city officers met they presented their idea. Tom Monahan assisted in getting a grant. The library was also a Carnegie library and received some funds from Andrew Carnegie. All this resulted in a new library being built. It remains a landmark today. The cost to build was a little more than $13,000.00.

Also, in 1904 excitement was created when news that the Liberty Bell, on display earlier in St. Louis, would travel through Arcola. Carried on the train in a special flatcar, it was on its way to Philadelphia. The train was scheduled to stop in Arcola for only five minutes. Townspeople knew this and they gathered in anticipation to see the bell.

After the train stopped, Riley Matthews went to the flatcar, "pulled out a hammer and gave the bell a whack." (We know of one crack . . . but another?) Matthews was arrested but was later released. No one could find a law against the hitting of a Liberty Bell.

RAGGEDY ANN DOLLS

Did you know that the "Raggedy Ann" doll's originator was born in Arcola? His name was John Gruelle. It is said that Mr.

Raggedy Ann and Andy

Gruelle's daughter, Marcella, found an old mop-haired rag doll in the attic of their home in Connecticut. When it was sold to someone who was fascinated by it, this led to the manufacture of the Raggedy Ann doll that would be loved by children everywhere. After little Marcella died, her father found that writing helped him to get over his grief. He wrote many Raggedy Ann stories that he had told his daughter at bedtime. His books were written with the "Gruelle Ideal," a belief that happy books were good for children.

John Gruelle's father was a close friend of James Whitcomb Riley and drew illustrations for many of Riley's famous poems.

During the early days of Arcola, Mr. Riley was a frequent visitor. A group of men during this time formed a club called the Dynamite Club. Members had fun playing jokes, especially on newcomers to town. Some were dunked in the slack tub at Jacoby's Blacksmith Shop, and Mr. Riley was one of those dunked. He took it in stride, however, and said it was the biggest splash he ever made.

An early resident of Arcola, W. J. Bradbury, who came in 1858, could recall when he was young that children didn't eat much candy. Sugar was considered a luxury, but chewing gum was plentiful. Bradbury and friends collected the sticky, chewy gum from tall resin weeds which grew in the area. At that time Indians lived on the outskirts of town, but they were peaceful and got along with the townspeople.

In those days people walked several miles just to visit and to help one another when assistance was needed. They got together for fun, such as sleigh rides in winter.

FIRST NEWSPAPER

The first newspaper in Arcola, *The Arcola Record*, was started in 1856 by the Sellers Brothers of Tuscola. Soon John Gruelle of Arcola purchased the paper and published it for 17 years.

Two other newspapers, *The Herald* and *The Artesian*, were also published. Years later these papers were brought together and published under the name *The Arcola Record-Herald*, and to this day the newspaper bears this name.

Has Arcola ever had a publication relating only to the broomcorn industry? It has, indeed. The publication *Broom and Broom Corn News*, first published in Arcola in 1912, was the first in the entire country to devote space regularly to the industry. Each week it has been read in about 20 foreign countries, as well as in America. (Only the name of the publication has been changed.)

Col. Cofer, mentioned earlier, became a farmer and visited his son in Tennessee about the same time the first newspaper was published in Arcola. His son worked in a broom shop, and the Colonel returned to Arcola with several bushels of broomcorn seed. When he planted 20 acres there he had no idea that Arcola would become Broomcorn Capital of the World.

After the famous Broomcorn Palace of 1898 and Street Fair, many residents of Arcola moved away. A reunion was planned, a homecoming with Thomas F. Monahan as chairman of the event. All the buildings in town were painted one color. Monahan had more than a thousand letters mailed to former residents inviting them to return for a visit. He provided entertainment, checked on acts from Chicago, St. Louis, Springfield, and DuQuoin. A big name band played each year. The Broomcorn Palace was the center of attention.

Arcola was the first city in the state to build a large dance floor and rent a tent half the size of a football field to cover it. Many other homecomings were held, leaving several years between them. The one planned for 1944 was called off due to World War II, and in 1945 a warehouse fire destroyed all the homecoming supplies.

Arcola loved entertainment. In 1902, to supply it, an opera house was built. People in Arcola today still love entertainment, and the annual broomcorn festival provides it.

Although my mother was unable to attend a broomcorn festival she said, "I can always be entertained when we have a family get-together." Actually, she entertained us. On one occasion when my grandson Bruce asked about the olden days I would have preferred that she answer him. At the time, however, she had laryngitis and could not speak. Her sense of humor was revealed in her "sign" language.

Drifting in Memory . . .
". . . it is a tonic for the heart
to drift in memory."
                    Ben Burroughs

PART THREE

"What was it like in the olden days, Grandma?" asked Bruce.

"In the early days of broomcorn," I began, "there were horse-drawn buggies and wagons, kerosene lamps, and pot-bellied stoves. The world didn't move very fast. There were few airplanes. If you were traveling farther than five or ten miles you would take a train. There were few paved roads, and very few automobiles. Dirt roads in winter were either frozen or muddy in the Midwest where I grew up. When cars would get stuck in the mud, sometimes a passerby in a buggy jokingly yelled, 'Get a horse!'"

"I guess horses could always be depended on," Bruce said. "Oh, didn't people have electricity?"

"Not for awhile. No televisions, no refrigerators, no automatic washers or dryers, no indoor toilets. My grandparents had a wind-up Victrola that could play records. I could listen to "Alice Blue Gown," "Auld Lang Syne," "My Wild Irish Rose," "Roll out the Barrel," "Tavern in the Town," "Bring back my Bonnie," and "When you and I were Young, Maggie.""

"In those days did people complain much?"

"Times were sometimes hard, Bruce, but there were few complaints. Most people didn't worry about 'keeping up with the Jones's.'"

"Did people have to hurry to get their work done?"

"Not really, Bruce. No one rushed around or checked their watch every few minutes. People had more time to enjoy their families, though they worked hard."

"Did parents punish their kids?"

"Parents were strict with their children and punishment was seldom needed. Children had chores to do, with little time to get into trouble."

"Did kids have any fun?"

"Of course. There were movies, and even without TV, children could amuse themselves. They often made up their own things to do. They didn't ask, 'What can we do now?' Parents took their children fishing, camping and to fairs, and special events that were suitable."

"Was there much crime?"

"There was a lot less crime, Bruce, than there is now. People were not into drugs like today. Since mothers usually didn't work outside the home they had more time to spend with their children. They knew their children's whereabouts."

"Did you have telephones in the country, Grandma?"

"Oh, yes. The operator was called 'Central.' We had to hand crank the tall phones on the wall. Instead of phone numbers, there were short and long rings. My parents' rings were two longs and one short. In an emergency, such as fire, injury, or illness, there was one long, long ring. People would listen in on conversations to know what was going on in the neighborhood. There were no private lines."

"Were there supermarkets?"

"No. There were general stores. No varieties of foods, like today. No convenience foods. We cooked from scratch. Prices were amazingly low compared to today's prices, but wages then were also low."

"Will you write all that stuff down, Grandma, and save it for me? Hafta' do my homework now."

"Okay, Bruce."

In the old days you could buy coffee, freshly ground at the store counter, for 25 cents a pound. The grocer, a friendly person, waited on you. He usually doubled as a butcher. From a cold back room he brought your preference of meat: a side of pork, beef, lamb, or veal. Placing it on a large, wooden chopping block, he'd ask, "How much?"

For 25 cents a pound or less you could buy bacon, rib roasts, pork chops, or leg of lamb. Ham, sirloin, or round steak were 30 cents a pound or less. Of course, farmers who had cows didn't need to buy milk, but for people who did, it was ten cents a quart in glass bottles.

Cornflakes cost eight cents for an eight ounce package, sugar five cents a pound, bread five cents (never more than ten cents) a loaf, butter 25 cents a pound, potatoes two cents a pound, onions three cents a pound. Eggs varied in price during the year, usually 30 cents a dozen or less. Of course, farmers who raised chickens seldom needed to buy eggs. In those days, whoever heard of cholesterol?

Eddie Cantor sang, "Potatoes are cheaper, tomatoes are cheaper; now's the time to fall in love." But $2.00 for a marriage license was not cheap. A one-carat diamond ring could be purchased for $143.00. Compare that to today's prices.

At the grocery store the grocer would give a piece of candy to children. Penny candies, including gumdrops, licorice sticks, and horehound could be seen in an enclosure with a rounded glass front. Candy bars were a nickel.

To eat out at a diner was quite reasonable. Steak and onions cost 25 cents, a three-pork chop dinner 30 cents, and a piece of pie was five cents.

To get a tooth filled cost one dollar, shave an' haircut 25 cents, and ladies hair bob thirty cents. You could buy a pair of boots for less than $5.00, and a pair of men's pants for $4.65.

The price of a Brownie box camera? Just $2.29 up to $4.49. Film (6 to 8 exposures) cost from 22 to 50 cents. Clara Bow cloche hats in Sears 1927 catalog were only 95 cents each. In the fall of 1994, I noticed an advertisement for a cloche hat (designer Frank Olive) at Lord & Taylor stores for $220.00. The ad read: " . . . can take you anywhere, even to Paris in the **twenties.**"

What about the price of furniture? An old Sears catalog (early 1900's) lists bedroom suites made of golden oak, three pieces, (bed, dresser and commode) for $14.75. A solid oak desk, finished antique, with three drawers and a drop table to write on cost $7.95. An upholstered couch with steel springs, in either corduroy or velour, 75 inches long, was $5.95. A parlor heater that burned soft or hard coal, depending on the size, went for $7.35 to $9.95. A highly ornamented hard coal, nickel trimmed, base burning heater cost $15.65.

In olden days barber shops were known for other services besides haircuts and shaves. According to "Great Grandfather's Occupations," in Eric Sloane's *America*, the barber used to be a surgeon. The doctor's office became a museum as well, with skeletons propped up in corners, and many strange-looking things in sealed glass jars.

Barbers were known for blood-letting. The red and white pole outside the barber shop represented a bleeding arm wrapped with white gauze.

We also learn in Eric Sloane's *America* that barber shop chairs had no arms, and a separate stool for the feet. Shaving mugs were identified with the owners' names. Ordinary customers had numbers. Wealthy and famous customers had mugs that were fancy, sometimes having coats of arms or embellished in color and gold leaf.

In the early 1900's babies were born at home, often before the doctor arrived. Dentists pulled teeth without deadening gums. There were no antibiotics, no air conditioning, no central heating, no stereos or TV, no microwaves and no computers. Women wore their hair long, with a big bun in the back.

Long golf knickers were called Plus Fours. Lace-up leather boots called Hi-cuts had a pocket knife sheath on the side. Button shoes were in vogue. Homemade soap with lye was hard on hands. Popcorn was a popular item to string on Christmas trees. Remember when popcorn was made on an open fire, using a covered metal box with a long handle and shaken directly over the fire? And children believed that if they stepped on a crack in the sidewalk it would break their mothers' backs. Crowds of young people went caroling at Christmas.

Farmers' wives dried fruits, including apples, peaches, and apricots. On the Fourth of July there were sparklers for girls and firecrackers for boys, with parents to assist. Farmers had horse or mule-drawn plows.

"Stubborn as a mule." I'm sure you've heard that expression. Many farmers made use of mules by the year 1900. That year more than two million mules assisted farmers to cultivate their land—to plow, to harrow. Hitched to wagons or buggies they brought people to town and to church. In mining states they pulled in timbers for ceiling supports and they pulled out cars loaded with coal. Mules could be stubborn, refusing to go forward, and it took a lot (a very lot) of persuasion to get them to move.

My father didn't have mules on the farm. His horses, Hans and Fritz, were loyal. They obeyed every Giddap, Gee, Haw, and Whoa. If it became dark before my father returned home from town in his wagon, he could let the lines loose and the horses would follow the road perfectly. This included a steep hill, at the bottom of which was a narrow bridge.

As you requested, Mother, I am including a glimpse of some of the events in our country while broomcorn flourished. Those who have relatives who raised broomcorn, and other old-timers who attend the annual Broomcorn Festival may relate to some of these happenings.

You have read in history books that the year 1776 marked American independence. That was after Benjamin Franklin introduced broomcorn to America. On May 10, 1876 the tower bell in Philadelphia's Independence Hall rang out in celebration of 100 years of independence. Joining in were church bells and the city's chimes, including the Liberty Bell. The opening of the Centennial Exposition drew large crowds. People arrived by horse-drawn street car, carriage, railroad, and steamboat.

Colonial relics exhibited included Washington's false teeth, Colonial Army uniforms, and the contents of a "New England Kitchen of 1775."

The late Eighties was an age of immigration. National symbols included the Statue of Liberty (1886) and Ellis Island (1892). There were anti-immigrant forces—the Ku Klux Klan and the Immigrant Restriction League. A federal law in 1882 banned entry of the Chinese for ten years.

In 1893 electricity began to replace steam as the main energy source.

Americans, in the late 1890's, became fascinated with magic and fantasy. The Wizard of Oz was created in 1896. Over the years it never lost its popularity.

On Inauguration Day in 1905, crowds lined Pennsylvania Avenue to see the President. Mother, you were a teenager when Theodore Roosevelt doffed his top hat while people shouted, "Hurray for Teddy."

THE ROUGH RIDERS

Forty Rough Riders, members of Roosevelt's Spanish American War regiment, moved alongside his carriage and acted as an honor guard. The song, "There'll be a Hot Time in the Old Town Tonight," rang out above the people's shouts.

Roosevelt brandished a "Big Stick" abroad and promised a "Square Deal" in our country.

When he took the oath of office he was wearing an unusual ring. It was given to him by Secretary of State John Hay, formerly one of Abraham Lincoln's private secretaries. Hay asked that Roosevelt wear it at his inauguration as he "was one of the men who most thoroughly understand and appreciate Lincoln."

Some people are surprised to learn that the phrase regarding Maxwell House coffee "good to the last drop" was actually coined by President Theodore Roosevelt.

In 1912, while William Howard Taft was president of the United States, New Mexico was admitted to the Union on January 6, as the 47th state. On March 12, the Girl Scouts were founded. On April 15, the British liner, Titanic sank, after being wrecked by an iceburg. Fifteen hundred people were lost. On June 4 the first minimum wage law was enacted in the United States.

In 1913 Woodrow Wilson was inaugurated President of the United States. The twenty-eighth president, he served to 1921. Also in 1913, the Sixteenth Amendment authorized income tax.

In 1915 people learned of the first major international exposition. San Francisco represented the Pacific Coast exposition. Also in 1915, the House of Representatives moved to adopt the Eighteenth Amendment prohibiting the manufacture, sale, import, or export of liquor in the United States.

The United States entered World War I in 1917 while Wilson was president, and the Armistice was signed November 11, 1918. For many years November 11 was called Armistice Day, then, later, changed to Veterans Day.

In 1920 women in the United States won the right to vote.

Field of Memories

In 1921 Warren G. Harding was elected President of the United States. The twenty ninth president, he served to 1923 when he died at age 58.

SPORTS

It appears that most Americans thrill to baseball. In the 1920's, while farmers were working in broomcorn fields, George Herman "Babe" Ruth became famous for his home runs. Called the King of Swat, fans cheered him as he hit 54 home runs in 1920, 59 in 1921, and a record 63 in 1927. People sang "Take me out to the ball game . . . buy me some peanuts and Cracker Jack. I don't care if I ever come back from the old ball game."

Buster Crabbe and Johnny Weissmuller set many world records during the Twenties.

The man who brought college football into the Midwest and Notre Dame? Knute Rockne. His team won 105 games and lost only twelve between 1919 and 1931.

When boxing moved into the sports spotlight there was Jack Dempsey and Gene Tunney. Joe Louis and Rocky Marciano were champions in their own right.

The generation who lived in the Roaring Twenties were sheiks and flappers: Women in short skirts wore lots of makeup and fake jewelry. Bobbed hair was in style, and cloche hats. Men wore baggy knickers, bow ties, hair parted in the middle, slicked down with pomades. There were saddle shoes, ukuleles, pocket flasks, rumble seats and necking, the Charleston, and auto racing. How 'bout flagpole sitting? Albert Lindholm of New York dared to sit on a flagpole 500 feet above the ground. Sayings included: Go fly a kite, the cat's meow, oh yeah? Furniture included fringed floor lamps and mohair sofas.

In the Twenties, while my mother was putting on overalls, getting ready to help my father in the cornfields, she began to sing an old song called "In my Merry Oldsmobile." In 1905 the Oldsmobile Company sent two cars on the first transcontinental trip by auto, from Detroit to the Lewis and Clark Exposition in Portland, Oregon. There were no paved roads. Cattle trails and mountain passes slowed them down, not to mention muddy roads. It took 44 days for the first car to finish the journey.

A noted composer of songs, Gus Edwards, wrote the song, "In my Merry Oldsmobile," but for the drivers who traveled to Portland it was no merry trip.

In those days automobiles were considered luxury vehicles by those who could not afford them. They resented what they called the "idle rich." Wealthy women indulged in fur laprobes. Goggles and "dusters" were in style. The *New York World* reported that "the automobile has developed into an expensive luxury for the man who does not need one." It was named the devil wagon.

We know that eventually it was endorsed by doctors, clergymen, and women, and finally, by 1939, this vehicle became, to many, a necessity. More and more people began to realize just how convenient a car could be.

In addition to the Oldsmobile, my grandfather spoke of "The Stanley Steamer," a car manufactured by the Stanley Brothers. Also, the Studebaker Electric vehicle, built by the Studebaker Bros. Manufacturing Company, became an item for conversation.

THE MODEL T

My grandpa Phillips didn't raise broomcorn on his farm in Illinois in the Twenties, but sometimes he **raised cane**. That was after he bought a Model T Ford.

When Henry introduced the Model T to the market in 1908, each car cost $825.00. Near the end of 1924 with mass production, the Model T reached its lowest price, $260.00 each. I think Grandpa probably bought his car at the latter figure, but the price of that black car, to him, was a lot of money. You may have read that Ford said, "You can get it in any color, if it's black." Ford wanted his Model T to serve the farmer, and it did. It was great for traveling on country roads,

"Ford"

going to town on Saturday, for visiting friends and relatives on Sunday, or just pleasure driving. Mr. Ford indicated that by making the car small and uncomplicated with interchangeable parts, it would be very easy to maintain.

The Saturday in July when I got permission from my parents to ride to town in Grandpa's new Model T with him and Grandma I was thrilled. My first car ride! My brother John, in grammar school and a year and a half older than I, said, "I haven't heard of anyone getting hurt while riding with Grandpa, but he drives kinda' strange."

Ignoring his remark, I dressed in my second best blue dress with matching bonnet that Grandma made for me and hurried to her house, more than a mile away. In those days no one was afraid and never locked their doors. And living on a farm seemed especially safe.

When I arrived at my grandparents' home, Grandpa was backing the Model T out of a space in his barn barely big enough to house it. The noise, to me like a threshing machine, caused chickens in the barnyard to cackle, squawk, and dart wildly about, seeking to escape the strange, noisy vehicle.

When the car engine died, Grandpa, a big man with a shock of black hair, got out of the car. He was perspiring.

"I ought ta' take it back," he grumbled. "Old Rattletrap."

I heard other descriptions and names for the car later: part goat, part burro, gasoline buggy. She was called Tin Lizzie, Jalopy, Flivver if she behaved. When she misbehaved she became Old Rattletrap.

I waited for Grandpa to crank the car. My brother had briefed me on how a Model T got started: "First, you hafta' set the spark on the steering wheel, then lift the hood to regulate the choke, then start to crank it, sort of a flip of the wrist for turning the crank. Watch out, though, as sometimes it'll kick. When the engine starts, go quick around the car, jump in before the car goes forward. It always moves a little."

I crossed my fingers and hoped that Grandpa wouldn't get hurt. John said sometimes when you are cranking and it kicks, you can get a broken arm.

Grandpa was lucky. Old Rattletrap started at the first try. Grandpa moved toward the driver's side of the car, stepped on the running board and reached inside the car and adjusted the choke.

Grandma insisted on riding in the back seat, so I climbed in the front. She shared space with an egg crate and a cream can. On the floor of the car three large chickens lay, their feet tied together, their mouths open.

"They're warm too," Grandma said.

Grandpa wiped sweat off his forehead with a large red handkerchief, then adjusted the throttle, a hand lever that "gives it the gas," and we were off.

The dirt road had many chuckholes and I think we hit them all. I began to bounce, and I could see Grandma, a petite woman, also bounce, sometimes hitting her head against the top of the car. She tried to steady the cream can. The chickens threshed about on the floor, letting out a series of squawks.

On my right we passed a partially wooded area that included several sugar maple trees. On our way to school in the Spring, my brother and I would stop and steal a drink from buckets into which sweet water dripped. Holes had been bored into the trees and a hollow plug inserted through which the sugar water slowly dripped into a bucket.

Now we were going up a steep hill. The car began to cough and wheeze. It chugged and rattled as Grandpa urged it on. I began to wonder if Old Rattletrap could climb the hill. Then I remembered my father saying that a Model T called "Old Liz" won in a world championship hill-climbing contest at Pike's Peak, and I knew we'd make it. When we reached the top a big dog barked at the car, came close and bit one of the tires, then ran alongside for several yards. Grandpa pressed the horn. The strange sound of honking sent the dog off the road, fleeing in terror.

We drove past the one-room schoolhouse where my brother and I attended. All eight grades were taught in that one room. Teachers were strict in those days. More about that later.

Directly ahead of us a man riding a black horse pulled to the side of the road. When his horse reared the man shouted at Grandpa, something I didn't understand, but he looked very angry. Just then a car behind us passed on the wrong side of the road, leaving a cloud of dust behind. I could taste the dust.

Finally, we reached a paved road about a mile from town. It was called the "hard" road. It ran east and west. Traffic in those days was light, but caution was necessary to enter. We needed to turn left. So what did Grandpa do?

He never slowed down, looked neither east nor west, zoomed onto the hard road and turned left. All the way to town it seemed as if we were flying, but later my brother said we were probably only going about 20 or 25 miles an hour.

From the time we left Grandpa's barnyard until we bounced against the curb in front of the A & P store in Newton, Grandpa kept the same speed, never once moving that lever.

I saw a sign on the store window that read "Coffee or Bacon 25 cents a pound. Bread nine cents a loaf." I looked forward to a free stick of candy from the grocer. My pennies would buy enough candy for myself and my grandparents, with enough left to give to those at home. I knew that Grandma, never idle, would use some of the money from the sale of the chickens, eggs, and cream to buy yard goods for aprons and bonnets. Leftover pieces would go into quilts that Grandma loved to make, and that I thought were so beautiful. Grandpa didn't always buy something, but he loved to sit on a bench in the courtyard and chat with people.

    I now knew what my brother meant when he said that Grandpa's driving was a bit strange. John also said, "If Grandpa ever uses the reverse gear (the one in the middle) as a brake, Old Rattletrap would buck like a rodeo broncho." Knowing Grandpa, I knew it could happen.

    Grandpa lived to be 89. His hair was still black, but Grandma's hair turned gray many years before.

    E. B. White wrote a book in 1936 titled *Farewell to Model T*. He wrote, "I can still feel my old Ford nuzzling me at the curb, as though looking for an apple in my pocket." I don't believe Grandpa was that attached to his Model T, though he did keep Old Rattletrap looking like new.

    Still in the Twenties, was a slogan "Keep cool with Coolidge." Calvin Coolidge, 30th President of the United States, was the son of a strict New England farmer. He was a solemn man, and frugal. Some wits said he "looked as though he had been weaned on a pickle." People, however, admired him and voted for him.

Who was presented with the Distinguished Flying Cross by President Coolidge? His single engine plane was called "The Spirit of St. Louis." People called him "The Lone Eagle." His real name was Charles A. Lindbergh, and his home was in Little Falls, Minnesota. His plane was so named because the city of St. Louis contributed to his flight across an ocean, a distance of more than 3,500 miles. It took thirty-three and one-half hours for that flight. In 1927, when Lindbergh landed near Paris at Le Bourget Field, more than 100,000 people welcomed him with cheers. The French called him "the man with a heart of steel and the body of a bird."

That famous flight meant the birth of a new era of world transportation. Thousands of Americans, during parades in New York and many other cities, cheered as he passed by. Now a hero, he was commissioned a Colonel in the American Air Reserve.

Who was president when the stock market crashed? Was it Herbert Hoover? Yes. He was the thirty-first president. During his first year in office the Wall Street crash of 1929 occurred. He was blamed for the resulting collapse of the economy. That year investors lost $40,000,000,000. Banks failed. You remember, Mom. You said, "A good thing we have our big garden." Many people lost every penny. Those who "couldn't take it" committed suicide. The government and President Hoover tried to convince the people that "prosperity was just around the corner." But there was no prosperity.

"Brother, can you spare a dime?" was often heard.

As a Quaker, Hoover passionately believed in peace. He determined to devote his life to public service. In semi-retirement he remained an ideologist for the Republican party. He volunteered to assist American tourists to leave war-torn Europe and then he volunteered to head the Commission for Relief in Belgium (1915-1919). This position brought him public attention as the "great humanitarian." It was only after the 1929 Wall Street crash that he lost this reputation.

Will Rogers, a national figure who appeared in more than 300 daily newspapers, said regarding the Wall Street crash, "We were the first nation in the history of the world to go to the poorhouse in an automobile." Will Rogers was a popular person, loved by many, and people were saddened when he died. While on a flight to the Orient with the aviator Wiley Post, he was killed in Alaska.

In the olden days newspapers not only contained news, they included comic strips. Some of these comic strips lasted for years. A couple are **still** going. They were the first things people enjoyed reading in newspapers. Is it the same today?

A favorite was *The Gumps*. It began in 1917. There was Andy Gump, the chinless wonder, his wealthy Uncle Bim, plain wife Min, and son Chester. Another favorite was *Gasoline Alley*, with Skeezix and his family, also, *Harold Teen*, teenager during Depression years. People enjoyed Al Capp's *Lil Abner and Daisy May*, *Winnie Winkle*, the breadwinner, and banjo-eyed *Moon Mullins*. There were new adventures of *Apple Mary* who later transferred into *Mary Worth*.

Families enjoyed *Dick Tracy*, *Terry and the Pirates*, and *Brenda Starr*, girl reporter. Popular for years was lovable *Little Orphan Annie* and her dog, Sandy. In 1933 her writer received the following telegram, "Please do all you can to help Annie find Sandy." It was signed by Henry Ford.

SOUNDS

In the old days there was less noise than in today's world. Sounds of travel by horse-drawn wagon and buggy, and by train continued from previous years. Church bells pealed on Sundays. Iron lids on kitchen stoves still clattered. There were barnyard sounds: roosters crowed, hens cackled, geese

Field of Memories

and ducks quacked, turkey gobblers gobbled, pigs squealed, sheep continued to baa. Cows needing to be milked mooed their discomfort. When the Model T Ford became available, it coughed, sputtered, and banged. There was no television.

The sound from the first radio came out of various shaped boxes made of wood. A small table model looked like a church. A tall, heavy model had a Victrola on top.

In 1920, KOKA Pittsburgh, Pennsylvania, broadcast the election of President Harding. Most people who listened used crystal sets with one or two earphones. A crystal set was used for a radio receiver. Mother, you said that broomcorn was doing well during this time. How exciting it was when we got our first radio.

There were imaginative sound effects created by simple, yet mysterious devices: a knock on the door; footsteps, soft, stealthy, or determined; Fibber McGee's closet; Jack Benny's "Maxwell"; the rasping door to "the Inner Sanctum"; the Lone Ranger's horse Silver's hooves (a pair of coconut shells slapping on a sound board).

And then there were the voices such as Will Rogers' Oklahoma twang and giddy Gracie Allen. There was also music from Dinah Shore, Kay Kayser and his "Kollege of Musical Knowledge," the Hit Parade, and opera direct from the Met.

Let's not forget drama on the radio. The *Lux Radio Theater of the Air* entertained with radio plays. There was *One Man's Family* with Father Barbour and the ever popular *Lum and Abner, Vic and Sade, Yoohoo Mrs. Goldberg* and the voice-changing teenager Henry Aldrich.

How many readers have heard of, or remember Amos and Andy, introduced to radio in 1929, and an instant hit? And George Burns, the famous and long-lived entertainer, who was never without his cigar. And who didn't enjoy hearing "Good night, Mrs. Calabash, wherever you are?" And "Duffy ain't here, this is Archie, the manager, speaking." Reference was often made to Jack Benny's 39 years. Everyone loved Little Orphan Annie and admired Jack Armstrong, the All American Boy.

People enjoyed Flash Gordon, and Dick Tracy, and the shows: *The Romance of Helen Trent, The Right to Happiness, Ma Perkins, Backstage Wife, Mary Marlow,* and *Just Plain Bill,* who went out with *John's Other Wife* Orson Wells' deep voice on radio gained popularity for him as *The Shadow*.

Early radio announcers would ask "Men, when you sit on a small chair do you have a big hangover? Don't despair. Get a MYRTLE GIRDLE and get to the seat of your trouble." Another ad went "Is your hair wavy, men? Is it waving good-bye? Try Jackson's No-Rub-Glo-Coat, then the shine on your dome will be the twinkle in her eyes." Then there was The Perkins Pickle Program. "Always remember our slogan, 'Perkins Gerkins for your Internal Werkins!'"

Does anyone remember radio's earliest crooner, Rudy Vallee? As a child, he loved the saxophone. He collected recordings of a famous player, Rudy Wiedoeft, and soon bought an instrument. By receiving instructions from Wiedoeft by mail, he taught himself to play. Later he formed his own famous dance band. His popularity, both in England and America grew.

In 1928 women swooned when they heard songs he composed such as "Vagabond Lover" and "Deep Night." In the fall of 1929 he and his band began to broadcast on the air.

When he became a producer, he ushered in stars of the stage to the microphone. These included Ethel Barrymore and Walter Huston, who did dramatic sketches written for radio. Favorites of radio audiences in the Thirties were Jack Benny, Bob Hope, Eddie Cantor, Jimmy Durante, Fred Allen, and Edgar Bergen. While in his teens Bergen discovered that he had a talent for ventriloquism. In college he performed with the dummy that gained great popularity for him.

Quizz programs were popular in the Thirties. Quizzes with weekly contests had jackpots that grew bigger from broadcast to broadcast.

A national favorite radio program was *Information Please*. It afforded radio listeners an opportunity to confound a panel of encyclopedia experts. Another program, *The Quiz Kids* included children ranging from age six to fourteen years whose mental powers fascinated adult listeners. They competed, on one occasion, against four Senators, with Supreme Court Justice Douglas presiding over the contest. He declared it a tie.

Sounds that people loved to hear in the Thirties included Kate Smith's "When the Moon Comes Over the Mountain," Bing Crosby's theme "When the B-b-b-blue of the Night meets the Gold of the Day," Ethel Merman's "I Got Rhythm," plus other favorites "Night and Day," "Smoke Gets in Your Eyes," "Easter Parade," and more.

Jeanette McDonald and Nelson Eddy were together in operettas. Fred Astaire and Ginger Rogers were popular singers and dancers who drew tremendous crowds whenever they appeared.

Remember when swing music was in? Big band orchestras played, including popular Paul Whiteman, Guy Lombardo and his "Royal Canadians," Tommy Dorsey, Benny Goodman, Artie Shaw, Louis Armstrong. There was romantic music, dancing cheek to cheek, the Samba, the Rumba, the jitterbug of young people, and the Big Apple.

MOVIES

Who was the actress in the Twenties known as the "It Girl?" Clara Bow, of course. She was the queen of the vamps. Another actress, charming and lovable, was Mary Pickford.

What actor was called a sheik? Rudy Valentino, with his slick hairdo, middle-parted, and his perfect tango was truly a sheik. Known as "The World's Greatest Lover," he was mobbed by women. However, back in Italy, his own country, he was just one of many.

Were there any popular comedies in the Twenties? Many would say that Charlie Chaplin was a great entertainer. He had an unforgettable face and a funny walk.

Later, during Depression years, Hollywood movies became more serious. And in the Thirties "God Bless America" was never considered as "just being sentimental." Americans were proud of their country. *Gone With the Wind* was one of the greats and still is. Other movies included Walt Disney's *Snow White and the Seven Dwarfs*, *The Sign of the Cross*, *Cleopatra*, *The Good Ship Lollipop*, Mickey Rooney in the *Andy Hardy* series, *Flirtation Walk* (Ruby Keeler), *Born to Dance* (Eleanor Powell), *Mr. Smith* (Jimmy Stewart), *Captains Courageous* (Spencer Tracy), and many movies with Claudette Colbert, Carol Lombard, Humphrey Bogart, and Clark Gable. Other

Clara Bow Hats

more serious movies included *Birth of a Nation*, *Ben Hur*, and *The Ten Commandments*

Movies were clean. Words like "Damn," and "Hell" were no-no's. Not so today.

John Wayne became a movie hero after World War II. Though he never served in the military, Congress authorized that he be honored for his "example" of American heroism.

One of my grandchildren once asked: "Grandma, was it any fun to watch movies without sound?"

"Well, Bruce," I replied, "people in the old days enjoyed them. Kids liked westerns, lots of action. Even though there was no sound, the actors and actresses' lips moved to dubbed in words that appeared on the screen. There were no color movies until the early Thirties. Then came Technicolor in 1935."

"How much did kids pay?" Bruce asked.

"You may not believe it, but kids could go to a movie on Saturday afternoon, see a western, and perhaps a double feature, for only a dime. There was always a cliffhanger to coax 'em back the following Saturday. Zane Gray was a popular author of westerns."

"Movies for a dime. Wow."

"That's right. Gray wrote *Riders of the Purple Sage*, among many other books. In later years writers of westerns imitated his style. His books are still popular."

"Grandma, TV sometimes has old movies. Do you remember the names of any actors or actresses in them?"

"I just happen to have a list, a long one though. Ask your mom and dad if they've seen movies that include any of these: Betty Grable, John Payne, Carmen Miranda, Caesar Romero, Harry James, Shirley Temple, Jackie Cooper, Carole Lombard, Charlotte Greenwood, Jack Benny, Spencer Tracy and Fredric March. There was Nelson Eddy, Jeannette McDonald, James Cagney, Joan Fontaine, Robert Taylor, Virginia Bruce, Marion Davies, Una Merkel, Harold Lloyd, Don Ameche, Milton Berle, Dick Powell and Ruby Keeler. And not to forget Bette Davis, Loretta Young, George Brent, Janet Gaynor, Alice Faye, Kay Francis, Ginger Rogers, and Jean Harlow. Also, Jimmy Stewart, Franchot Tone, Buddy Ebsen, Wally Beery, Bob Hope, Jane Withers, Bing Crosby, John Barrymore, Fred McMurray . . ."

"Gee! Sure a lot of 'em. But I gotta go now. I think **you'd** best ask mom and dad."

Great shows in 1935 included, among others, Eugene O'Neill's *Ah Wilderness*, *Our Town*, *The Petrified Forest*, *You Can't Take it With You*, Clifford Odets' *Golden Boy*, and Orson Wells' *Macbeth*.

My mother often mentioned happenings in the Thirties that included

Amelia Earhart the famous flyer. Miss Earhart accomplished many firsts. She was the first woman to receive the Distinguished Flying Cross, and the first woman passenger on a transatlantic flight. When she attempted to circle the world, however, she failed, vanishing at sea somewhere in the Pacific.

Another event that brought headlines in newspapers for some time was the kidnapping in 1932 of Charles A. Lindbergh, Jr., the manhunt and the Hauptmann trial and conviction.

In 1933 the Twenty-first Amendment repealed National Prohibition. There would be no more "dry" days.

On March 4, 1933 Franklin Delano Roosevelt, age 51, took office as President of the United States. The Depression had not gone away, but many people were optimistic that Roosevelt, though afflicted with crippling polio, could somehow help the country out of its problems and protect the common man.

Metal braces on Mr. Roosevelt's legs made it very difficult for him to walk, but he did walk to the podium to accept his nomination as President. His nomination speech will long be remembered:

> "I pledge you—I pledge myself to a New Deal for the American people. Let us all here assembled constitute ourselves prophets of a new order of competence and of courage. This

is more than a political campaign; it is a call to arms. Give me your help, not to win votes alone, but to win in this crusade to restore America to its own people. **The only thing we have to fear is fear itself!**"

This last sentence became the hope of the American people. They believed that prosperity was soon to come. Famous for his fireside chats, he closed a speech with the following:

> "You must have faith; you must not be stampeded by rumors. We have provided the machinery to restore our financial system; it is up to you to support and make it work. Together we cannot fail."

Roosevelt's New Deal was put in action within one hundred days after his inauguration. The Civilian Conservation Corps (CCC) put millions of young men to work in road building, flood control and forestry. To administer federal relief projects the WPA (Works Progress Administration) emerged. There were other organizations—including the Agricultural Adjustment Act to regulate farm output. (Mother wondered if corn would come under that category.)

The Social Security Act was passed to aid the aged, widows and dependent children, and the unemployed.

The year after Franklin Delano Roosevelt took office as President, the

Dionne quintuplets were born to Elzire Dionne: Annette, Cecile, Marie, Emilie, and Yvonne. Their arrival on May 28, 1934 thrilled many people.

On May 7, 1937 headlines in newspapers shouted that the Hindenburg, the largest airship ever built, burst into flames as it neared its landing in Lakehurst, New Jersey. When its hydrogen-filled gas bag exploded, hundreds of spectators watched in horror as burning bodies plunged to the ground. More than 800 feet long and 135 feet in diameter, the Hindenburg had made 36 passenger flights across the Atlantic. A total of 36 persons were killed, and many of those who survived were disabled.

Mother, I have mentioned some of the events in our country while broomcorn grew. Another, that you asked to briefly tell about, includes World War II.

In the Thirties people became militant against war. College students went on peace strikes. Peace was preached in many places. However, in 1937 President Roosevelt warned that the world was moving toward a war. In 1939 the clouds of war rained down. On September 3, 1939 Neville Chamberlain, in a speech to his people, said, "This country is at war with Germany." That was the beginning. It was months before action began. Then Hitler went on a rampage. More countries became involved, and many bloody battles fought. Hitler overran six countries in three months. In America young broommakers were given draft deferments in order to make corn brooms that were badly needed by the War Department to clean military camps overseas.

Victory gardens supplied food for many families during the war. Farmers worked extra hard to produce food to feed nations and their armies.

Benjamin Franklin said, "There never was a good war or a bad peace." Your history books tell in detail about World War II, and the sneak attack on Pearl Harbor.

On June 5, 1944, General Eisenhower, chosen Supreme Commander of the Allied Expeditionary Forces during World War II, told his AEF that "The tide has turned. I have full confidence in your courage, devotion to duty and skill in battle. We will accept nothing less than full victory! Good luck! And let us all beseech the blessing of Almighty God upon this great and noble undertaking."

From all directions the Allies now moved against Berlin. Finally, after more than five and a half years, the world celebrated V-E Day on May 8, 1945.

Following World War II, broomcorn production slowed in several states. Many farmers switched to other crops.

My father continued to grow corn, but not the kind without ears. And there was hay to be put into the hayloft. Like his neighbors he arose early and worked until sunset.

Field of Memories

𝔇𝔬𝔴𝔫 𝔬𝔫 𝔱𝔥𝔢 𝔍𝔞𝔯𝔪
𝔇𝔲𝔯𝔦𝔫𝔤 𝔅𝔯𝔬𝔬𝔪𝔠𝔬𝔯𝔫 𝔇𝔞𝔶𝔰

PART FOUR

My mother would have enjoyed the humor in Mark Twain's definition of a farm. He defined it as consisting of a creek for swimming, a hayloft for sleeping, outbuildings for exploring, and an assortment of haystacks to relax in. More than likely, however, mother would have wanted to add the word "work." It did take work to mow the sweet-smelling hay and bring it to the hayloft.

When father had finished mowing I used to watch him in his wagon as he passed through the barnyard gate with Hans and Fritz, our horses, pulling the heaping load of hay that was headed for the barn.

Besides a barn and house, many of yesteryear's farms had other buildings. There might have been a smaller barn, a springhouse, a woodshed, and sometimes an ice house, a milkhouse, or even a blacksmith shop. Farmers had carriage sheds, privies and chickenhouses.

In his book regarding early America, Eric Sloane wrote: "... all civilized America was farms and all Americans were farmers . . . The lessons that a farm teaches are, after all, not reserved for rural life . . . . Everything in those days came the hard way; work was never finished."

Mr. Sloane stated that in early America people were held together by the common bonds of farm life. Whether you were a blacksmith, a carpenter, a politician, a butcher, or a banker, you were also a farmer. Having a rural background and a farming philosophy in those days was a necessity. George Washington and every member of his first Congress farmed with their own hands. They believed that farmers were "a brotherhood of husbandry which knew neither politics nor class." And can you believe that Benjamin Franklin, whose public affairs kept him away from agriculture, bought a 300-acre farm?

We know that Mr. Franklin introduced broomcorn to America, though at the time he wasn't aware that the plant growing in his yard was broomcorn.

Unlike earlier farmers, my parents didn't have many extra buildings besides our house and barn. Nevertheless, this did not decrease greatly the amount of daily work.

During broomcorn days our family rose early in the morning. I can almost hear my mother's voice calling to my brothers who were still asleep.

"Get up, get up! Chore time. Your father is already outside . . . ."

Morning and night chores took some time as we had horses, cows, sheep, pigs, and chickens to attend to.

Since my father was the first one to rise he built a fire in our wood-fueled cookstove, put the teakettle on to heat water, and often made baking powder biscuits for breakfast. Sausage, gravy, and sometimes hot cereal accompanied the biscuits, or freshly churned butter and sorghum molasses. When strawberries were ripe in our garden we enjoyed them with sugar and fresh cream.

After breakfast was over and dishes done, I went upstairs to make beds. Making the soft featherbed that my brothers slept in took some doing. Oh, the hills and valleys that formed after lying on it. It required a lot of banging, patting, and smoothing to even it up. I was tempted to just fall over on it and nap awhile. My broomcorn broom seemed to beckon, however, so I used it to sweep the rug in the front room. (Some called it the parlor.)

Like Alice Page, for many years Garden columnist for the *Santa Barbara* (California) *News Press*, my parents "grew up in the olden days of hard work and love and simpler ways."

A song comes to mind when I remember the chore of milking our cows, "Can she milk a Jersey cow, Billy Boy?"

I tried to learn to milk Bessie when I was about age 10, with instructions from my brother John, but when she turned in my direction, rolled her big eyes and lifted a hind leg (getting ready to kick me I was sure), I ended my lesson. John teased me for being afraid.

"What kind of farmer's wife will you be when you grow up?" he asked.

"Well," I replied, "how do you know I'll marry a farmer? Besides, I might even be an old maid!"

OUR CREAM SEPARATOR

Every morning my father and one of my brothers carried large pails filled with milk into our kitchen. Soon the milk would be separated into skim milk and cream. I loved to watch this being done.

The cream separator was a hand-operated machine with a big steel bowl (about four gallon capacity) on top of the machine. The purpose of the separator was to remove the cream from the milk. Into this bowl dad poured the whole milk. He then began to hand crank the separator. It made a humming sound. The longer and faster it was turned, the louder the sound.

My brother Walter explained that the milk flowed by gravity into a packet of cone-shaped discs (about 50 discs) inside a metal case. The discs were separated by a fraction of an inch. Milk flowed from the bowl into the center of the pack of discs which rotated at a very high rpm by the hand-cranked machine and a series of gears that made the discs and case rotate at high speed. This would throw the skim milk to the outside and allow the cream to come out an opening in the center. Two spouts, one for cream and the other for skim milk lead to separate containers.

The process was repeated with more whole milk being poured into the bowl until all the milk was run through. Metal parts of the separator that were used had to be taken apart and washed.

Because we had no refrigerator nor icebox, we placed cream and butter in a bucket and, using ropes, lowered them into our deep, cool cistern. Before the milk was separated mother always reserved some whole milk for drinking and to use on cereals. We never used skim milk for drinking. It was taken outside and poured into a trough for the hogs.

We purchased ice at an ice plant in town to make ice cream. Some people cut huge blocks of ice from ponds in winter and stored them deep in sawdust to keep frozen during the summer.

In broomcorn days we churned our own butter. Mother poured cream into a churn, a tall container (larger at the bottom) with a lid, and a dasher in the center. After lifting the dasher up and down, up and down for several minutes the fat particles would separate from the liquid, leaving bits of butter and buttermilk. The bits of butter were worked into a solid mass. We had a butter mold made of wood that imprinted a fancy design on the butter when it was pressed into the mold. Later, we had a metal churn with a crank that would get all the butter from the cream in about ten minutes.

A substitute for butter that many people still use is oleo margarine. The original color of margarine was white. A capsule containing coloring came inside the package when purchased and the contents could be mixed into the margarine to make it resemble butter.

OUR COOKSTOVE

Cooking during broomcorn days without gas or electricity, with no supermarkets and no convenience foods, was time consuming. Our cookstove was heated by wood from trees cut down on our farm and sawed into firewood. The stove had a firebox on the upper left-hand side underneath the cooking surface. Below the firebox was a container for ashes. Ashes needed to be removed frequently in order for the stove to operate efficiently. Dad and my brothers cut wood to a size that fit into the firebox.

"Keep the woodbox filled," mother would tell my brothers.

Wood stoves have flat cooking surfaces. Most have six eyes or round openings with iron lids. The size of the lids can vary or be the same size. You cannot regulate the heat under the eyes. However, since temperatures vary, you can move cooking utensils backwards and forwards to obtain the temperature needed.

The oven is heated from the left and the top of the stove by heat circulating from the firebox. When baking you need to maintain a constant oven temperature. In early days stoves had no heat indicators. To test the oven temperature some cooks laid scraps of white paper in the oven. They could determine the temperature by the amount of time it took to brown and scorch the paper. If the food browned too quickly a piece of brown paper would be placed over the top of it to prevent the crust from burning.

Mother would test the oven temperature with her hand. Just by placing her hand in the oven for a few seconds she knew whether it was too hot or not hot enough for whatever she would bake. Bread and big yeast biscuits (rolls) were her specialty. She often used starter yeast, shared with a neighbor. For school lunches she bought loaves at the grocer's as the slices of "bakers' bread" held together better than homemade bread, and bread wrappers came in handy.

On mother's baking days, while walking home from school, I could smell bread baking long before I reached the kitchen door. Taking it fresh from the oven, mother would break off the delicious crusty heel, smile, and say, "If you want jam it's in the cupboard."

With freshly churned butter, however, nothing else was needed for that tasty snack.

A warming oven attached to the top of the stove was handy to keep food warm until everyone could sit down to the table.

To facilitate cooking food in a hurry, mother would remove one of the iron stove lids over the fire area and set a utensil—usually an iron pot, directly over the fire. When less heat was needed she moved the utensil farther back on the stove toward a reservoir. A pan of sour milk set back in this manner could eventually become cottage cheese. After pouring off the liquid the remaining solids were put into a cheesecloth bag and hung up to drain. Voila! Cottage cheese.

On the right side of the stove a reservoir that held several gallons of water kept the water warm whenever the stove was in use. Without a dishwasher we used boiling water from a teakettle to rinse the dishes after they were washed by hand. We also used boiling water to sterilize canning jars. Without detergents it was difficult, if not impossible, to remove soap scum from dishwater no matter how hard we tried.

My father installed a hand water pump in our kitchen which brought water from a cistern just outside the house. We used this water for everything except drinking. Dad hauled drinking water in barrels from a well a few miles away. Mother drank a lot of water, and we often saw her using a longhandled dipper to dip water from a pail in our kitchen.

WASH DAY

Without electricity, wash day seemed to last forever. Mother used a washboard to scrub laundry. (Later we purchased a hand-operated machine with an attached wringer.) Made of corrugated glass, the washboard was set in a wooden frame with two six-inch legs and set down in a tub of hot water. Mom laid articles to be washed across the washboard and rubbed soiled spots with a cake of brown lye soap. She spent hours bending over the washboard, scrubbing clothes that included greasy, grubby overalls for my dad and brothers. Soap, scrub, slosh—then rinse in another tub of water, and wring by hand.

White clothes, especially towels, sheets, and underwear, were boiled in a washboiler of water on the cookstove. Finally, mother hung everything outside on a clothesline to dry. In summer, fruit-stained dishtowels were spread on the grass to be bleached by the sun. In winter, clothes froze and some were not dry by nightfall. Long underwear took on a ghostly appearance at night.

We heated water for bathing in a wash boiler on the cookstove. A large, round metal tub substituted for a bathtub. Saturday night was bath night, with daily sponge baths. (Some called them spit baths.)

Why Saturday night for baths? It started with the belief that the Sabbath began at sundown on Saturday and should be a time to follow the adage that cleanliness is next to godliness. So that was when people bathed.

IRONING

We ironed clothes that had been previously dampened, with irons called flat-irons or sad-irons. Boat shaped and smaller than an electric iron, they were placed on the hottest part of the cookstove surface above the firebox. It was necessary to change irons often and to wipe off any soot from the bottom of the iron. To iron without getting a black smudge on white or light colored clothes was difficult. White shirts were the worst. No wonder people called them sad irons. They were that, indeed. We found, however, that by running the iron over paraffined paper it helped to clean the iron and make for smoother ironing.

FRUIT PICKING

Blackberries and dewberries grew wild on our farm. The worst part of picking berries was the pesky chiggers. They had a mean bite. But mother's pies made from freshly picked berries, as described by my father after a long day in the cornfield, were "scrumptious and larripin," and worth a few chigger bites.

My brother John and I picked cherries for cherry pies from trees that grew near our grandparents' house. One day, while picking from branches high in the tree, my grandfather began to sing, "The higher up the cherry tree, the riper grows the cherry . . . the more the boys do court the girls the sooner they will marry."

We also picked peaches, plums, and apples. Whenever I picked apples I thought of the story of Johnny Appleseed. His real name was Jonathan Chapman. Because of an unhappy love affair he became known as an eccentric. He always travelled barefoot, carried a supply of apple seeds and a Bible. He wore a tin pan on his head which he used for cooking when he became hungry. When he planted apple seeds in town where he travelled, people were kind to him.

One day in 1847, after walking twenty miles, he stopped in Fort Wayne, Indiana at a friend's home to read his Bible and to leave a supply of apple seeds. Here he died. He was seventy-two years of age.

Mother canned many jars of fruit and vegetables. Her goal was to have all her shelves in the basement filled. Usually she canned 300 quarts each of fruit and vegetables every year, not to mention meats, pickles, jams, jellies, and apple butter. But oh, the heat in the house in summer during canning time after having a fire in the cookstove for hours. It took a long time to process many of the foods.

Summer evenings, after my father returned from work in the cornfields, we had a late supper and later gathered on our front porch to enjoy a southerly breeze. Dad brought his pipe to smoke, "to keep the mosquitos away," he said. He and mother sat in the creaking porch swing and discussed the day's happenings while children chased fireflies, or played hide-and-seek. A bright moon and millions of stars looked down as crickets carried on a never-ending chorus.

Sometimes summer storms with lightning flashing and thunder booming brought sheets of rain to cool the air and quench thirsty fields of corn.

Mother did a lot of mending, but seldom did any sewing. In early broomcorn days sewing machines were operated with foot pedals. Many women made their own clothes and clothes for their children. How scandalized people would have been to see a woman wearing pants. Mother, however, welcomed the new style when it was introduced. She loved to be out-of-doors helping with any outside chores—caring for her White Leghorn chickens, working in the fields with my father, even shucking corn.

RECREATION

People enjoyed square dances, card games, checkers, horseback riding, horseshoe pitching, ice cream socials, and taffy pulling. (The boy would choose the girl that he wanted to pull candy with.) Women enjoyed quilting bees. They often affixed names of their friends on the quilts. There was hunting, fishing, and baseball. During corn husking, women helped one another cook dinners. This could go on for several weeks while work in the fields was in progress.

There were spell downs at school. Box suppers were held in the schoolhouse. At a box supper, when a young man was the highest bidder on boxed foods, (for example, a pie) his reward allowed him to share it with the young lady who brought it to the supper. Sometimes this resulted in the beginning of a romance.

Marbles, called Aggies, Immies, Lobes, or Cabiolies, were fun to play with. On Halloween boys used to swat each other with long black stockings filled with flour. Kids threw snowballs in winter, played hide and seek, and blind man's bluff. In addition to buggies and wagons, many farmers owned sleds. Some farmers improvised, using detachable runners to put beneath wagon wheels. What fun to ride in a sled over the snow!

In the fall we gathered walnuts, hickory nuts, and, after a frost, persimmons. Before a frost these small persimmons were puckery and not fit to eat.

SCHOOLS

Attending school in a one-room schoolhouse in early days was not uncommon. The teacher taught all eight grades in this room. Children would listen to the recital of classes other than their own, though they pretended to be studying. (Teacher wasn't fooled.)

A large heating stove helped to keep the room warm in winter. A small cloakroom was provided to hang coats, hats, and to leave lunchpails—and in winter for overshoes on the closet floor.

Sometimes children played ball during the noon hour. Recess was short. Boys usually grouped together, girls in another group, with lots of chatter and giggling. Punishment for being naughty usually meant staying after school and writing on the blackboard with chalk whatever the teacher ordered—sometimes a hundred times. School ended early in the spring so that children could help parents with chores during planting time in the fields. This time was made up by starting earlier in the fall.

It was about four miles to high school from my parents' home. My brother and I left the house at seven o'clock in the morning for the long walk. In winter we wore long underwear as sometimes the temperature hovered around zero. Pulling long stockings over the underwear took some doing. It was necessary to fold over the underwear legs at the bottom and ease the stockings on.

TOILETS

In the olden days there were no indoor toilets. There were portable containers kept in a bedroom and used as a toilet, called chamber pots. Outdoor conveniences called privies, built some distance from residences and schools, were wooden structures containing a long, wooden seat in which holes were made, set over a pit. You would likely see a Sears, Roebuck catalog instead of toilet tissue. Sometimes, on Halloween night, boys thought it fun to tip over these structures. Parents, however, weren't too happy.

A company called Chic Sales built outhouses with a quarter moon cut out of the door.

Although the olden days had many inconveniences, there were plenty of pluses such as clean air to breathe, and one could clearly see the stars, like little candles, at night. People didn't lock their doors as nothing was ever stolen or vandalized while they were away.

People knew and helped their neighbors. If a farmer became ill before he finished planting his crop the neighbors completed the work for him. People didn't **want** so many things during broomcorn days, and there were fewer inducements to buy things. No TV commercials. No credit cards. Day or night, one could take long walks without fear of being held up or molested.

Chores always had to be done by children before play. Drugs and violence were rare. Parents taught their children self-discipline, to respect people's property and the rights of others. Children obeyed their parents.

In olden days there was less stress and fewer broken homes. To honor your parents meant you would live a long life and things would go well for you.

There was joy in simple things such as seeing the sun rise and set; watching little lambs frolic like happy children; baby chicks, soft and fuzzy creatures and a delight to hold; green fields of corn that indicated a fruitful harvest; a table set with love and healthy foods, vegetables, meat, and fruit, all from the farm and shared with loved ones.

Most farmers were descendants of the peasants of Europe and desired to stay in agriculture because they enjoyed it. However, many were forced to leave, due to huge losses. Machinery and fertilizers were costly, and Mother Nature could be cruel.

In the mid-Twenties and Thirties, farmers like my dad labored from dawn until dark preparing the soil, planting, cultivating, and finally harvesting their crops.

Sometimes the Embarrass (pronounced Am-braw) River overflowed its banks and ruined my father's crops in the rich bottomlands. In other years corn perished in the fields due to lack of rain. Heavy rains in late spring meant late planting, and late harvest was a risk for farmers. It was truly a gamble.

Like his neighbors, dad believed that farming was similar to a card game. They didn't always win, but when they were dealt a poor hand they always played it well. They looked forward with hope to a new year. When corn plants were healthy and grew "knee high by the Fourth of July" farmers' spirits rose.

During the Depression in the Thirties my parents and others used the barter system. Dad hauled cords of wood from our farm to pay doctor and dentist bills. There was little or no money. By selling chickens, eggs, butter, and cream, groceries such as coffee, sugar, and flour could be purchased.

After my parents moved to town, my father, a gentle, honest man, now age 70, still worked hard and took pride in the fruit of his labor. One day in April 1950, he began to spade a small garden plot, preparing a lettuce bed. His heart, weakened by many asthma attacks on the farm, failed. He preceded my mother in death by more than thirty years.

John Ruskin wrote, "To watch the corn grow, or the blossoms set; to draw hard breath over plowshare or spade; to read, to think, to love, to pray—these are the things that make men happy."

How wonderful when the American heritage consists of leaving the children of each generation something good to cherish—something other than money to influence their lives.

In a large Spring catalog received from Gurney's Seed & Nursery Company, I noted an advertisement for broomcorn seeds. Other seed catalogs may also have them. The caption (in Gurney's) below a picture of broomcorn:

Field of Memories

"Great for Crafts.
Produces top quality straw
for brooms. Grows 4-5 ft. tall—
like corn without the ears.
Makes a fine privacy screen.
Birds relish the mature seeds.
Approx. 750 seeds per packet.
110 days."

For those who have a plot of ground and would like to experiment with planting broomcorn seeds it could become an interesting project.

Broomcorn seeds always bring to mind Benjamin Franklin and the time he planted a seed in his Philadelphia garden, unaware of its identity.

Broomcorn Nostalgia

Field of Broomcorn, Oklahoma
(from Oklahoma State University)

*There's a time to plant
and a time to reap.*
(Ecclestiastes)

PART FIVE

Mother did I tell you that Benjamin Franklin, who introduced broomcorn to America, visited me in a dream. He wanted to know more about the plant that grew in his Philadelphia garden, later known as broomcorn.

MR. FRANKLIN:
They say that curiosity killed the cat, but since I'm already, er, on reprieve for a short time, I'd like answers to some questions about broomcorn. I know things have changed . . . and I've forgotten since the 1700's. You may call me Ben.

ANSWER:
You probably want to know about growing and harvesting broomcorn.

Mr. F.:
 Yes. Suppose that I'm a broomcorn seed. Can you take it from there?

A.:
 If you were a broomcorn seed, the person who selects you would need to keep in mind that you must be clean. This is necessary to keep the crop pure, free from smut. Machinery is used for seeding. The stand should be uniform to secure good quality brush. Brush is defined as the seed heads of broomcorn. These seed heads when mature are the important part of the plants.

MR. F.:
 What is my goal?

A.:
 Your goal is to eventually have the seed head of your plant made into some type of broom or whisk broom.

MR. F.:
 What kind of soil is best . . . ?

A.:
 You can grow in almost any kind of soil, but deep, alluvial soils usually produce a higher yield and quality of brush. Much of the broomcorn in the past has been grown on rich riverbottom land. My parents had such land.

MR. F.:
   When should I be planted?

A.:
   Planting depends on your location. It may be between April first and July first. The earlier the crop is sown the sooner it will be ready for harvest. Whoever selects seed should know the varieties of broomcorn.

MR. F.:
   How many varieties . . . ?

A.:
   There are three main groups: standard, western dwarf, and whisk dwarf. Standard broomcorn usually grows from seven to 15 feet high. Its brush is used in making all types of brooms and whisk brooms. This brush is from 16 to 24 inches or more in length. The "handle" or stem of the brush, cut at harvest, is eight inches long or more and strongly attached to the stalk. The brush is usually pushed entirely out of the boot (the sheaf) by lengthening of the stem at heading time.
   Western dwarf can attain a height between four to seven feet. The brush is from 15 to 24 inches long, is weakly attached to the stalk, and can be pulled or jerked at harvest time—usually without cutting. Brush of this variety is also used in making all types of brooms and whisk brooms.

MR. F.:
And whisk dwarf?

A.:
It usually grows to a height of two and one-half to four feet, and produces a slender brush about 12 to 18 inches long. The stem is easily detached from the stalk because of several creases or constrictions near the bottom where it joins the stalk. Whisk dwarf broomcorn, like western dwarf, is harvested by pulling or jerking. Its brush is used for making whisk brooms and occasionally for the insides of floor brooms. I hope this isn't boring you.

MR. F.:
Not at all. How do you control weeds and insects?

A.:
To control weeds your plant needs to be cultivated. Cultivation, however, should be shallow to avoid injuring your roots.
The same insects and diseases that attack other sorghums will also attack your plant. Recommended control measures are the same.

MR. F.:
What about harvesting?

A.:
> You will be harvested either by cutting or pulling, usually depending on whether you are standard or dwarf as I mentioned. Your brush turns from pale yellow to green before maturity. Harvesting should not be done until the entire brush is green from the tip down to the knuckle. If harvested while the lower ends of the fibers are still yellow they will be weak and flabby at the bottom. When your brush is ready to harvest, the seeds are usually in the milk to dough stage.
>
> (In European and South American countries broomcorn is usually harvested after the seeds are mature, and are used for feed, e.g., swine.)

MR. F.:
> Does my brush ever change color?

A.:
> Yes. About four or five days after the proper harvesting stage is reached your brush begins to get overripe and starts reddening. The seeds firmly attach themselves to the branches. Because of this seed characteristic you were able to find seeds still attached to the whisk broom that you used to clean your hat.
>
> Your brush doesn't increase in weight after the seeds reach the milk stage. All of the later growth goes into the seeds.

MR. F.:

Is there much hand labor required during harvest?

A.:

Yes. About 10 to 14 days of hand labor is required to harvest, cure, thresh, and bale a ton of cured brush. A ton of brush contains about 40,000 to 70,000 heads. Each brush or head must be cut or pulled separately by hand. In subsequent operations your brush is handled in handfuls or small armfuls—with care taken to avoid tangling the fibers. The necessity of doing the work promptly requires the use of large crews. As mentioned earlier, migrant workers called canaries assisted in the harvest.

MR. F.:

Yes, they came to the Arcola area in spring.

A.:

Farmers' wives didn't sing like canaries when they had to cook three meals for ten to forty hungry men. These men often collected their pay each day and spent their wages at night gambling and drinking.

MR. F.:

Did they continue to do this?

A.:
No. When fields of corn grew smaller, neighborhood helpers drove in, bringing their lunch . . . . Now, we will talk about tabling.

If you are standard broomcorn and cut from the stalk, most of the crop is "tabled" or broken before it is cut, but some is harvested with a corn binder. Because you are tall it's necessary to bring your head down for easy reach in cutting.

MR. F.: (chuckling)
Rather violent! What is tabling?

A.:
Tabling consists in walking between two rows of broomcorn and breaking or bending the stalks diagonally across each other, forming a so-called "table" of the two rows, with the heads extending out beyond the rows forming the edges of the table. The table is formed at a height of about two and one-half to three feet. Usually the tabler walks backward, facing the table as it is formed. Sometimes, however, he walks forward and breaks the stalks behind him. Ordinarily, the harvester cuts your brush from the stalks immediately after tabling two rows across the field.

Cutting requires two or three times as long as tabling. Cutting is done with a special broomcorn knife.

Broomcorn Nostalgia

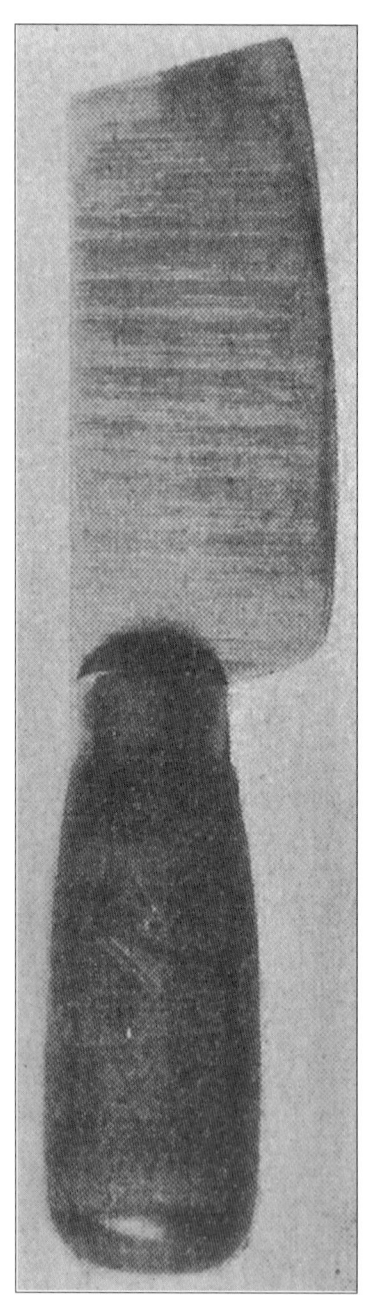

Broomcorn Knife

Field of Memories

MR. F.:
Can you describe how this is done?

A.:
The harvester grasps your brush in one hand and pulls the stem against the blade of the knife at the point on the stem where it is to be cut. By pulling the brush against the knife blade, and exerting an outward pull at the same time, the brush with the handle or stem can be withdrawn without cutting entirely through the boot or sheaf. A bit tricky! The boot must be pulled from the stem at the time of cutting if it is accidentally cut through.

As soon as a handful of your brush is gathered it is thrown on the table in small bunches. These bunches, which are of convenient armfuls for loading on a wagon, are placed only on alternate tables. The table on which your brush is piled is referred to as a "lay-on." The other on which no brush is laid is called a "lay-off" table.

Let's take a break now and have a piece of Broomstick Cake. It's delicious.

MR. F.: (after the break)
What color should I have?

A.:
To be the best quality brush, you need to have a bright pea-green color and be free from discoloration. You will then bring the

best price when marketed. Dwarf varieties contain varying proportions of reddened fibers. This indicates poor quality. Coloring material in broomcorn plants formed when the stems, leaves, or heads are injured by insects, mechanical abrasions, excessive moisture, or over-maturity (as mentioned) can cause reddening. If crops are rotated, incidence of disease and insects is reduced.

Sometimes your brush is stained or discolored by mold, exposure to rain, or contact with the ground, or by being "burned" in the shed, rick, or bale. These discolorations affect the market value of the brush. They can be removed, though, largely by bleaching and dyeing. Oh yes, it is necessary that brush be cured.

MR. F.:
   Am I ill?

A.:
   No, not from an illness. Quick drying helps to retain the bright green color of your brush.

After your brush remains on the table in the field 24 hours or **less**, it is usually hauled to the curing shed. In case of rain the piles are turned over on the table as soon as the tops of the piles are dry. Generally, the longer your brush is left in the field the more quickly it can be cured in the shed. However, if left on the table in the field **more** than 24 hours your brush is likely to become bleached.

MR. F.:
Earlier, you said that I would be threshed. Do I deserve punishment?

A.:
When a few loads of your brush have accumulated at the curing shed your brush is threshed to remove seeds. It's then placed on slats within the shed to cure. We'll learn about this later, in conjunction with baling.

MR. F.:
How long does curing take?

A.:
Curing requires about 10 days to three weeks, depending on the weather, the dryness of your brush, and the thickness of the layer placed on the slats. Brush is usually placed on slats at a depth of two to four inches, depending upon the amount of moisture content. Slats are placed so that air is allowed to move freely across the layers; if piled too thickly your brush may become "shelf burnt" or discolored due to heating. There may be some reddening. When brush begins to heat it should be re-shelved to prevent further damage.

MR. F.:
What happens if the crop is not tabled?

A.:
In that case, the bunches of brush either are thrown on the ground or upon stalks which have been broken over, or else they are placed in between two stalks in a row so as to hold the brush off the ground. Your brush often remains in the field for several days, or longer, before it is hauled to be cured. Curing is completed in ricks where it is left until dry. Then it is threshed and baled in one operation.

Curing of your brush in ricks saves considerable labor and expense, but involves a much greater risk from weather. However, under favorable weather conditions rick-cured brush may be of excellent color and appearance, especially if the crop is ricked rather promptly after cutting and the ricks are well built.

MR. F.:
How are ricks built?

A.:
Boards, stalks, or the ground serve as a base to form the ricks. Your brush is placed on the base with the tips out and stems inward and overlapping the middle. Brush laid lengthwise keeps the middle full and ties in the sides. The ricks, three to five feet

tall, are tapered toward the top like a teepee. At the bottom they are about four feet wide.

MR. F.:
    And then?

A.:
    There is baling. This consists of pressing brush into a compact bale weighing approximately 350 pounds. Broomcorn must contain sufficient moisture to avoid damage during baling, yet be dry enough to store safely. In order to secure uniform and compact bales of brush, care is necessary. No rugged or uneven bales. Tangled brush can easily be seen in the bale. Bunches of brush must be butted carefully on a flat surface such as a table, box, or barrel before being handed to the man in the baler, and this man also must be careful when laying down the brush. If your brush has the seed end outward it detracts from the appearance of the bale. Baling is usually done by custom balers and bales sold to broom manufacturers.

    Broomcorn is "processed" (sorted by length and grade) before it is delivered to the broommaker. In the old days, according to Thomas Monahan, Jr., broomcorn was all sold in the raw state or in large bales. Today, 99 percent of broomcorn goes to the processor. The processing operation was originally done by the broomshop.

Mr. F.:
   And now?

A.:
   Now it is done by professional processors. They separate the corn by length and grade. Then they sell it to a dealer such as The Thomas Monahan Company. The dealer resells the broomcorn—but only the length and grades that the manufacturer wants.

MR. F.:
   Is baling ever done at the same time as threshing?

A.:
   Yes, sometimes. Two balers are occasionally used with one thresher. Brush then can be placed in one baler while the bale is being tied in another. This permits continuous baling. If there is only one baler the bunches of threshed brush must be placed on the ground while a bale is being tied, and then again picked up and put into the baler.

MR. F.:
   Is it better to thresh before or after curing?

A.:
   It's of better quality when threshed before curing because fewer of the fine

branches are knocked off by the thresher when brush is moist and flexible. All brush that is threshed before curing is cured in sheds or on racks, and some brush is shed cured before threshing.

MR. F.:
Are there machines for threshing?

A.:
Yes. Power machines for threshing have two cylinders that rotate in opposite directions. Brush is carried past the cylinders by a toothed chain. In the next step the seeds at the tip of the brush are knocked off first, but as brush is carried toward the far ends of the cylinders the chain runs nearer the cylinders and the remaining seeds are removed.

It is important that practically all seed be removed from your brush. In order to remove the seed, the brush at the butts or tips is evened and laid straight before being fed into the thresher.

MR. F.:
What is done first when harvesting and threshing broomcorn?

A.:
The usual procedure is to start the entire crew in tabling and cutting brush in the field. After the first tables have been

cut, the brush is hauled and dumped in front of the shed. The custom thresher comes to the farm during the afternoon or evening, or perhaps the following morning, and the entire crew except the haulers is called in from the field to assist with the threshing. The hauling continues until all or most of the harvested brush has been brought from the field and threshed,

When threshing is completed, the men resume the harvesting until the thresher returns—perhaps the following day.

Women would spend many hours preparing dinner (served at noon) for threshing crews. The story is told of a farm wife who was expecting threshers for dinner, but whose family had failed to provide her with wood that morning to cook the dinner. Her husband left for work and when he and the entire threshing crew arrived hungry at his home for the noon meal the table was laden with food. However, **nothing had been cooked**. Raw meat, raw potatoes, pies ready for the oven . . . .

MR. F.:
What happened then?

A.:
The husband, assisted by hungry threshers, hurriedly gathered wood and after some delay all sat down to a delicious meal.

MR. F.:
I expect the woodbox was kept full after that.

A.:
That's right! After harvest, fields in the semiarid regions of the United States have sometimes been used for forage as livestock pasture. In France the stalks are used for paper pulp. (Escourrou 1959). The pulp is used in the manufacture of newsprint paper, and fiberboard.

MR. F.:
What about marketing?

A.:
In most cases marketing was done from the farmer to the broker or the dealer. The dealer then resold the broomcorn to the broom manufacturer. Very little of the corn in later years was sold to the manufacturer.

Mr. F.:
What was the dealer's function?

A.:
The function of the dealer was first to give the farmer cash and store the broomcorn; and second to have broomcorn with the desired characteristics that each broomshop wanted.

Mr. F.:
Please explain.

A.:
By storing large quantities in a warehouse, a manufacturer could visit and pick the bales he wanted from several different farmers. If he dealt directly with the farmer he would have to take all of the broomcorn grown by the farmer.

Mr. F.:
Even if he didn't want it all.

A.:
Right. If there were a lot of short bales in the field he would be buying short broomcorn when he only needed long warehouse corn. Conversely, he could be getting fine fiber from one farmer when he needed heavier broomcorn. It wasn't practical for a manufacturer to tour every farm before he found the right broomcorn.

Mr. F.:
So?

A.:
So, the procedure was to bale the broomcorn. The dealer would then look at the corn and the farmer would sell it to the highest bidder—usually a dealer. The dealer would then receive the corn in his warehouse

and the manufacturer, at his convenience, could come to the warehouse and look at the corn in storage as I believe I mentioned. By picking exactly what he wanted, usually from three or four different farmers, he could soon be on his way.

Mr. F.:
Did a broker ever take a manufacturer to the field to inspect the crop?

A.:
Yes, on occasion. If the manufacturer bought the corn, the broker would charge a brokerage fee and take care of paying the farmer receiving the broomcorn and arrange for shipment of the broomcorn to the manufacturer.

Mr. F.:
This saved time, yes?

A.:
Yes. It allowed the manufacturer to return to his plant rather than spend a long period of time in the field.

Mr. F.:
Is there any classification of broomcorn in marketing?

A.:
Yes. Brush is classified roughly according to whatever its use will be. For

example, that known as "insides" or "handle corn" is usually short—sometimes stemmy—and is used for making the inside portion of a broom.

MR. F.:
Are horses used in the labor of harvesting?

A.:
Yes. Except for the substitution of tractors instead of horses to pull wagons—and power threshers—the labor of harvesting is performed in much the same way as it was in pioneer days.

MR. F.:
Being an inventor when I was around many years ago, could I have been of any assistance?

A.:
Most likely, you could have been. The hurl cutter machine removed brush from the cornstalks. After that came sizing machines and power winders. Inventors have improved the hurl cutter, but a harvester machine for harvesting broomcorn isn't used in the United States or in Mexico. It still takes tedious manual labor.

According to a letter received in June of 1994 from Dr. H. H. Hadley, agronomist at the University of Illinois, regarding his development of a variety of broomcorn that can be mechanically harvested, he writes:

> "I have (developed) two kinds that are uniformly 3 to 4 feet tall, with brush of adequate lengths. One is not ideal, however, in that the brush does not get out of the boot. The biggest problem is that an ideal harvester has not been developed.
> Mechanical harvesting is a two phase process:
> (1) get the brush bundled and deposited at a brush processor and
> (2) processing the brush from bundles to sorted fibers (by length)—dry and ready to bale.
> Mr. Tim Monahan of Arcola, Illinois thinks he has the 2nd phase solved.
> We can still develop better harvestable types than we have, but what we do have can help solve phase 1. These types have to compare favorably... with the current leading variety, Deer..."

Dr. Hadley and Dr. Woodworth developed and released Deer about 26 years ago. It is high quality, high yielding, but seven feet tall and not adapted to mechanical harvesting.

Because of the high cost of hand labor to harvest broomcorn, the crop in the United States is almost non-existent.

MR. F.:
Where does it grow?

A.:

Corn is the outstanding crop of Mexico. In some sections of Mexico it is said that broomcorn will grow and develop even without rain during the growing season.

MR. F.:
No rain needed?

A.:

In most arid areas in Mexico, according to Thomas Monahan, Jr., there is irrigation. Broomcorn will make a crop on less moisture than any other crop. It does, however, need rain or irrigation. Irrigation is usually a pre-water, then once thirty days afterward and then once sixty days plus or minus after the planting. In Colorado the average rainfall was only 11 inches per year and yet they can get by on much less than other crops. Therefore it's desirable to grow.

Mr. F.:
How about fertilizer?

A.:

It also takes a little less fertilizer, and isn't as hard on the soil as some other crops.

MR. F.:

Thank you for all the information. I must return now.

A.:
You're welcome. And **thank you for introducing broomcorn to America.**

If Benjamin Franklin had a broom made from broomcorn in his home, he could have known that "a new broom sweeps clean." In Parts Six and Seven we will learn many interesting things about brooms.

Broomcorn Nostalgia

Broomcorn Curing Shed

Field of Memories

Tabling Broomcorn

Broomcorn Nostalgia

Cutting from the Table

"A New Broom Sweeps Clean"

PART SIX

When mother received a new broom from the Newton Broom Company, she once asked, "How do we happen to call brooms by that name?"

There are two theories. Some people contend it's a corruption or coinage from the word "besom." The prophet Isaiah mentions bezom, which is its first historical mention, and in some countries the broom is still referred to as bezom.

Bezom is a shrub which still grows in England and elsewhere. It bears large yellow flowers, but the twigs are tough and flexible, and when bound together and fastened on a stick they are used as a broom.

One of the pioneer manufacturers of brooms, Mr. A. F. Weymer from Syracuse, New York, didn't accept the Bezom theory. He said, "To broom means to splinter. For example, if you chew the end of a match until the fiber is loose you broom the match. When driving piles, if the top of the pile is shattered or splintered, you broom the pile. Iron rings are used on the end of piles to prevent brooming. Is it possible that the first hickory brooms were made by splintering the end of the hickory stick? This process known as brooming and hence the name broom was used for the hickory splint broom . . ."

THE AMANA COLONIES

Ever hear of a blind broommaker?

Philip Griess of the Amana Colonies made brooms, though blind, long before 1932 when the Amana Colonies people voted to change from a communal society to free enterprise.

In making brooms, visual impairment is no handicap. Many blind persons worked in broomcorn factories and were proud of their skills.

The Amana Colonies had their own broommakers, as well as persons who excelled in other crafts and arts. They made floor brooms, outdoor brooms, whisk brooms, brushes, pot brooms for the kitchen, and others.

From Germany, these people of West German, Swiss and Alsatian ancestry journeyed to Ebenezer, New York, where they settled. In 1854 they left New York for

Iowa. Here they founded seven villages, encompassing 26,000 acres. Each member contributed some particular skill handed down from father to son, in true Old World tradition.

The Amana Colonies are a registered National Historical Landmark and have been placed on the Hiawatha Pioneer Trail.

In 1971, Mr. and Mrs. Norman Schanz decided to revive the broommaking craft in the Amana Colonies in West Amana, Iowa, using the old hand-operated machinery which was built with walnut, cherry, and maple woods. The machinery was made available to them by William Leichsenring, who had obtained it from Philip Griess.

At Ye Olde Broom and Basket Shop in West Amana, brooms are made to order while the customer watches their creation. The equipment used is nearly 100 years old.

An Illinois farmer, Ted Hocking, used one-hundred-year-old machinery to make brooms. He indicated that broommaking has been his hobby. Mr. Hocking and his grandson Tim of Mt. Carmel, Illinois, started out in 1976 with a small garden plot of broomcorn, never dreaming they would be swept into a broommaking enterprise. After harvesting their broomcorn they weren't sure just what to do with it. However, they took it to a broommaker who was about to retire to have a few brooms made. Instead, the broommaker gave them his century-old equipment, but made them promise to keep

Ye Olde Broom and Basket Shop, West Amana, Iowa. Mr. and Mrs. Norman Schanz, owners.

broommaking alive in Wabash County, Illinois.

Ted and his grandchildren, Tim Hocking and Cindy McGee, set up shop in a barn and a shed on the bank of the Wabash River and began to produce brooms, about 500 a year. They even made a "cobweb" broom with very long bristles in order to reach high ceilings.

The family purchased much of its brush from a supply firm since their crop was not sufficient to make enough brooms to satisfy their customers.

Area residents were anxious to purchase the "Hocking" brooms which were produced in three sizes: a kitchen broom, a large warehouse broom, and a small child's broom. All were of high quality. People often waited more than a year to obtain one. (The Hockings admit they could have produced more brooms, but then it wouldn't have been a hobby.)

Another broommaker, Frank Hrupsa, 78, has been making brooms at his home near Mustang Corner, Delaware, on a steady basis for 10 years, as reported by Theresa Humphrey, *Associated Press*, in December, 1993.

Miss Humphrey stated that Mr. Hrupsa plants broomcorn on a quarter-acre plot on his large farm. After harvest he makes the brooms in a workshop next to the plot. His father, an immigrant from Czechoslovakia, made a cruder device by running a stick into a bunch of broom straw . . . and using a nail to hold it in position.

The son paints or varnishes the broom handle after the brooms are made and Hrupsa's name etched in the wood.

Over the years, Hrupsa has made several hundred brooms. By visiting craft shows and festivals he sells and demonstrates broommaking. He doesn't sell brooms to stores.

At this writing, according to the *Associated Press*, he still enjoys operating the large combines on his 500-acre grain farm, run by his sons.

This industrious gentleman has kept alive the state's ties to its colonial past, and he indicated he expects his son Frank to carry on with broommaking for many, many years after his death.

BROOM MANUFACTURERS

Manufacturers of brooms are able to obtain brush tied in bundles or bales on order. A ton of broomcorn will make approximately 1,000 brooms.

DYEING

The brush has already been processed in shops, sorted by hand and cut by machine into exact length of fibers. The bales are dyed in large vats. Thomas Monahan Jr. states that, in general, all broomcorn is dipped in a very light green dye. It is a cold dye that is used to standardize the color of the corn. After it is dipped it is immediately taken out of the dye. Hence, the dye only gives it a green cast. Ninety-five percent of all broomcorn is dipped in this light green color. It is made to match the natural green. If the corn has been sun bleached it helps to bring back the original green.

After dyeing, the wet brush is often bleached overnight in a closed chamber with sulphur dioxide produced from burning sulphur. This may fade the dye slightly, but its purpose is to make the color more uniform and to remove red stains and other discolorations on green fiber.

Various types and grades of brooms are made from the different qualities of brush. The best brooms are made from a good, fine brush having plenty of round branches or seed fibers. Coarser brush may be used in making others.

Warehouse brooms are made from long, coarse brush. They are used in stores, warehouses, factories, steel mills, smelters, cotton mills, garages, basements, barns—areas where big brooms are needed for special purposes.

Short brush is used for the inside portion of the household broom, and many factories use substitute fibers, particularly in their "sale" brooms. Short brush is also used for whisk brooms, toy and hearth brooms. Whisk brooms, being small and short handled, are used for brushing out cars, closets—any areas too small for a household broom. Toy and hearth brooms are usually simply made, though you may find attractive and unusual ones on the market. The toy broom market is seasonal, being greater at Christmas time. However, the use of small brooms for general household duties and for fireplaces has somewhat increased.

If brush is damaged, crooked, knurled, or badly stained, it is not used in manufacturing brooms and is discarded.

MAKING BROOMS IN A FACTORY

Though steps vary in different factories, the following is a fairly accurate explanation of how brooms are made.

To start making a broom a winding machine (winder) is used. It is a turning lathe with a hole large enough to hold a wooden handle. Different kinds of brush lay in piles within reach of the operator as he stands near the winder. He clamps the wooden handle in the lathe toward one end. Then the end of a spool of wire is nailed to the handle and several rounds of wire under tension are wound onto the handle.

Next, as the handle turns slowly in the winder, handfuls of brush are fed evenly under the taut wire which binds the brush close to the handle. Short brush and poor grades of brush known as "underwork," "insides," or "handle corn" are used. After sufficient insides have been added, the short ends of the fibers extending above the wire are trimmed off as the handle rotates.

The shoulders of the broom are then formed by winding on bunches of brush called "covers" or "turnovers" on opposite sides of the broom. More brush is wound on at these points, but with the fibers in the opposite direction. These fibers are long so they may be turned down to form rounded shoulders. Then a layer of good long cover fiber is applied around the broom, followed by a finishing layer of hurl. The wire is nailed to the handle and cut off.

The fiber above the wire is trimmed and covered with closely wound wire or a piece of velveteen cloth to enhance the appearance of the broom. The fibers tend to sprangle at this stage and are held together with a loop of twine which is slipped down over the handle and around the hurl.

The brooms are given a final "scraping" to remove loose fibers, stems, and seeds. The brooms must be dried. This is done in some factories before stitching. While clamped in a shaping mold the broom is stitched with three to five seams of colored twine in a sewing machine. Then the brooms are trimmed to the desired length. Instead of stitching, a band of heavy wire is often used on warehouse brooms to hold the brush in place.

Labeling the brooms covers the lathe marks and wire-end on the handle. Before being bundled or boxed in units of one dozen for shipment the brush is usually covered with a sleeve of paper.

Household brooms are being made without shoulders and with little or no hurl on the outside to compete with synthetic brooms and imports—primarily from Mexico.

Plastic brooms have competed with the corn broom but the reason a corn broom sweeps better is that **many invisible hair-like fibers on the broomcorn stalk hold the dirt better than any other type broom.**

NEWTON BROOM COMPANY

Many years ago, when broomcorn was plentiful in Illinois, wagon loads of it were brought in from local areas to the broom factory in Newton to be made into brooms. Not today, however. Broomcorn fields have been replaced with soybeans, and the Newton Broom Company purchases its broomcorn through a dealer, The Monahan Company, who obtains it mainly from Mexico.

Formerly the factory, which has been in operation more than sixty years, had employees who sorted and graded the brush, each stalk being put into a bundle for a specific use. Now bales are purchased with the crop already sorted and graded. There are different lengths for different type brooms: warehouse, housebrooms, and a cheaper broom. "Bear grass" is used in this latter broom. It grows as a broad leaf plant in the mountains of Mexico, brought down by burros, and shredded in shredder plants in Mexico. Then it is used at the factory as fiber for promotional brooms, a leader item or special.

According to Anna Rohr, who worked for the broom factory for more than 25 years, there were five broommakers when she started work. Prior to that time, however, there were ten. Many changes and additions have been made. Since then storage buildings have been constructed and ownership of the broom company has changed. Anna has now retired.

In 1980, 500 to 600 dozen house and warehouse type brooms were manufactured every month, some sold locally, others out of town. Thirty-two people were employed at the factory, including eight broommakers.

The factory has a variety of cleaning equipment, including mops and brushes, and for a sideline they have added Soft Sweep magnetic brooms. Plastic fiber brooms and deck mops are assembled here. A dryer with no flame was purchased as well as an $8,000 stitcher machine.

Until recent years broom handles were purchased from outside suppliers. The factory painted most of the handles using an air-operated machine. An electric machine applied a coat of sealer. A dipping process was used to paint the handles, the handles being dipped into a tank one at a time. After a rolling operation in a machine the painted handles were dried. This process, however, has now changed.

According to Becky Shamhart of Newton Broom Company, handle painting is now done on a horizontal unit with the handles running over three lengthy belts until dry. All handles, now imported from Indonesia through brokers, are re-sanded.

Seven broom winders are employed and about 120 dozen brooms made daily. Since the $8,000 stitcher machine was purchased there are now three additional air-operated stitchers, thus improving production and quality.

Although other buildings in nearby locations have been added, the broommaking, painting, drying, sewing, and trimming are still done at the same original location. The office, likewise, has not moved.

One plant is used for the slipping and finishing of brooms, mop winding, and packaging of items added over the past few years. All outbound shipping is done from this plant which has three loading/shipping docks.

In 1991 a new warehouse in another location was built, strictly for storage of raw material. All inbound broomcorn, grass, handles, yarn, and raw goods come into this warehouse. This new building also has three power-operated landing/shipping docks.

The plant which I visited in August 1994 is spread into five different buildings with a total of 38 full-time employees. Most production is piece work, with stiff regulations on quality and a full-time quality control inspector. In 1993 sales totaled nearly four million dollars.

Another broom company in Illinois is France-Merkle, in Paxton. More than a million brooms are produced here annually.

A California broom factory, The National Broom Company in Stockton, had 54 employees. Tours of their factory can be arranged. Their address is 24 West Scotts, Stockton, California 95203; phone (209) 948-9351.

BROOMCORN STANDARDS

Are there broomcorn standards? Yes, there are. Certain standards for broomcorn were informally drawn up and recommended by the Bureau of Agricultural Economics, U.S. Department of Agriculture, effective March 1, 1931. Though seldom adhered to closely, they served as a guide and provided definition of terms.

The standards include quality, grade, class, and division designations. Quality is determined by color, size, length of fibers, defects of the individual panicles A, B, C, D designations, and apply to both hurl and underwork divisions of broomcorn, except that Quality A brush must be all hurl. The grades of brooms are: Choice, Good, Medium, Common, or Sample. Classes of brooms are: Whisk, Parlor, Warehouse. The Divisions are: Hurl, Self-working, and Underwork. An example of a grade designation: "U.S. Good Parlor Hurl."

The processed grades, according to Thomas F. Monahan, Jr., are:

1. A pea green color with perfect fiber.
2. A slight blemish in color, or slightly heavier fiber, or a combination of both. However, it is still good solid broomcorn that will work into a good quality broom.
3. Slightly stained or heavier fiber corn. It is still usable, with good sweeping characteristic.
4. Anything not defined regarding the three grades above. Since this is a product of nature there is some looseness in the definition.

The other point is the processing quality. No more than five percent stems and eight percent shorts are allowed in any processed hurl. All inside stalk should be two inches or less. Seven percent above this is to be the standard.

In following pages, superstitions of long ago concerning brooms will be revealed. And we learn of the many uses of brooms and broomsticks.

Ever bake a Broomstick Cake? The recipe is given.

Broomcorn Nostalgia

Making Brooms with ANCIENT MACHINERY
Photos by *The Gazette Co.*, Cedar Rapids, Iowa

1. Getting ready to wire broomcorn straw to the stick.

Field of Memories

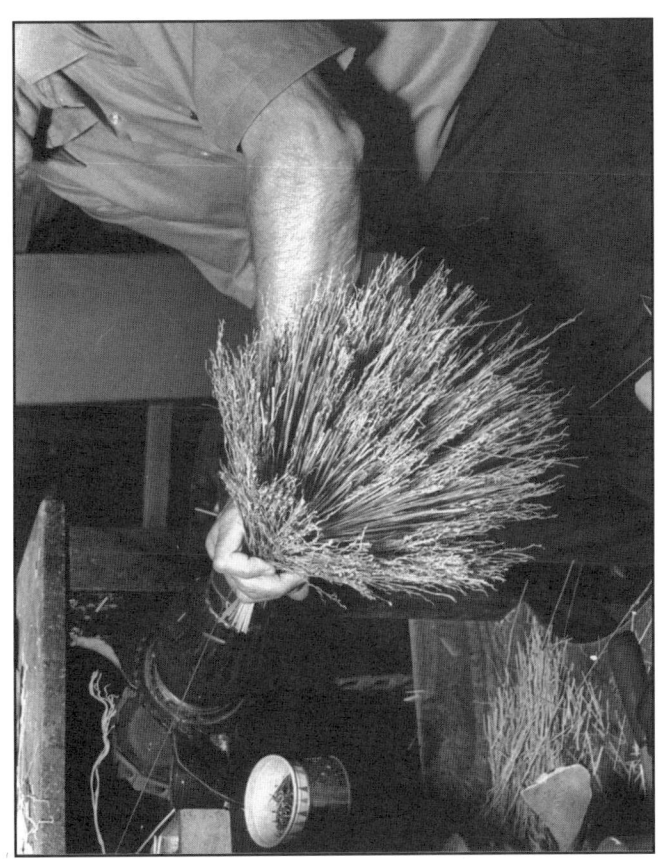

2. Wiring a handful of broomcorn to the stick.

3. Trimming straw with sharp linoleum knife.

4. Hammering straw to get moisture out.

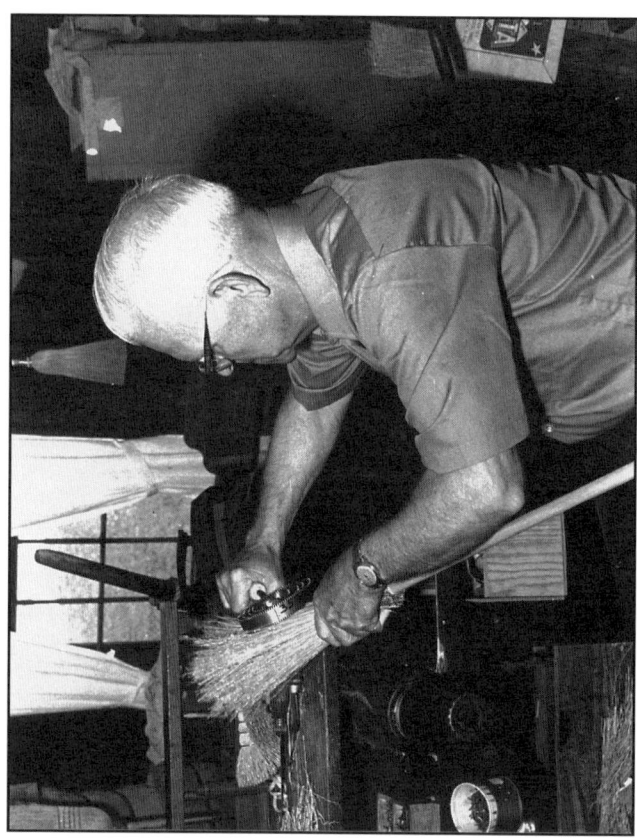

5. Using curry comb to get seed out.

6. Broom is placed in a vise for sewing.

7. Final Step: Handstitching the broom.

Field of Memories

> *"Variety is the spice of life"*
> *(Proverb)*

PART SEVEN

BROOMS AND SUPERSTITIONS

Hundreds of years ago people believed that brooms were the vehicles of witches. They also believed that brooms could work magic. In New England the broom was the traditional mount of old-time Salem witches. In Saxony it was considered very unfortunate to be struck by a broom as the person struck would surely die of consumption.

Sophisticated people today don't believe in superstitions—or, do they? Do you walk around a ladder instead of under it? Walking around it is safer, you say, since you don't want something to accidentally fall off a ladder on the roof on your head, such as a hammer or a bucket of paint.

Here is another superstition concerning brooms. If a girl stepped over a broom, or if someone swept under her chair,

Witch riding a broom

Field of Memories

it was a sign of bad luck, and that she would be an old maid. Of course, nowadays old maids are career-women.

If a broom fell outward from the door it was a sign of callers soon to arrive. To meet broom sweepings in a doorway was unlucky.

If, after sweeping the rug, the broom was accidentally left in a corner, strangers would surely visit the house that same day.

To drop a broom was a sign of visitors—and to see a broom that was worn straight across was the sign of a firm mind in the user.

To lend a broom was bad luck. (No doubt, especially if it was never returned).

Superstitions are not as prevalent now as they were in the past, for example, who believes that witches ride brooms on Halloween? You do?

USES OF BROOMS

The following poem, author unknown, tells of various uses of brooms.

> "Aunty keeps her broom handy—no plug-in is needed.
> She finds many uses and each has succeeded.
> She sweeps the sidewalk and also, she said,
> "I can push things out from under my bed."
> When she spies a cobweb on the ceiling somewhere,
> Aunty bats it away with 'nary a care.
> When her corn broom wears out, the handle she saves

for her broomstick dance—it's sure to bring raves."

Brooms may be used for sweeping light snow and cut grass from sidewalks, or to aid in getting old leaves out of ivy or flower beds with no danger to plants. They can be used as props for snowmen, as gifts for kitchen showers, for cleaning fireplaces and floors, and to complete a witch's costume for Halloween. They are good as a sales gimmick to display items for sale, and whisk brooms are used at baseball games to brush dirt off home plate.

Ever use a broom to exercise? You could lose a few pounds, but not get as thin as a broomstick. To reduce hips and waistline and help shape your legs, try a "stomping" exercise. Synchronize your leg movements with the sweeping motions of your broom. As you pull the broom back, lift your leg and bend at the knee. When you pull the broom down in a sweeping motion stamp your raised foot hard on the floor. (If you live in an upstairs apartment, perhaps wait until the downstairs tenant is out.) Do this alternately with left and right legs.

An exercise for inner thighs: With feet apart, stand with weight evenly distributed on each leg. Holding a broomstick for support, bend knees (keeping back straight). Go down as far as possible. You should feel your inner thigh muscles working. Return to starting position. Repeat 25 times.

In a letter to *The New York Times* in April, 1993, Elizabeth R. Turner of Oakland, California writes:

> "I have discovered what I call the Art of Sweeping and practice it upon my kitchen regularly. It is an ancient movement that women especially have performed since the days of child rearing in the cave. I choose music to fit my mood and begin my dance across the floor with the broom. I enjoy the full-body workout that it gives me, as well as the ordering of priorities that seem to result from this intentional meditation. I choreograph it fresh each time, moving the dirt sometimes in a circular fashion, at other times in parallel or diagonal lines. I have always felt that there was something spiritual about sweeping, as opposed to scrubbing, mopping or scouring, which require aggressive frenetic action. Perhaps with so little time to be at home, it is all the more important that housekeeping be performed at the level of an art form."

If you performed any of the movements mentioned above, you have probably worked up an appetite, so why not bake for yourself and family a Broomstick Cake? Here is the recipe:

BROOMSTICK CAKE*

*It's a mystery how this name originated. Perhaps the recipe was envisioned while someone was hungry after doing broomstick exercises. Also, ingredients in the cake; apples, walnuts, and molasses, suggest the fall of the year when brooms are made.

1 egg; 3/4 cup brown sugar; 2 T. melted butter; 5 med. size cooking apples; 1/2 cup margarine or butter; 2/3 cup granulated sugar; 1/2 cup walnuts, chopped; 1 cup molasses; 2-1/2 cups flour; 1-1/2 tsp. baking soda; 1 tsp. cinnamon; 3/4 tsp. ginger; 1/4 tsp. cloves; 3/4 tsp. salt; and 1 cup hot water. Prepare an 8 x 12 x 2" pan (I use a glass pan) with melted butter (2T.) and sprinkle brown sugar over the butter evenly.

After peeling and coring apples, cut them into approximately 1/2-inch thick slices. Arrange slices over sugar mixture. Sprinkle with nuts. In a bowl, cream butter and sugar. Add egg and molasses, mixing well. Stir dry ingredients into creamed mixture until smooth. Add hot water and stir again. The batter will be thin.

Pour batter over apples. Bake at 350 degrees for 35 minutes, or until cake tests done. Remove from oven. Loosen cake around the edges and let stand 5 minutes before turning out on serving tray. (Eat only a small piece now if you are watching your weight.) Makes 8 to 10 servings.

USES OF BROOMSTICKS

If you need an extra clothes pole in your closet, try a broomstick. Is your stepstool not handy? Use a broomstick to get unreachables off closet shelves. And in your garden, broomsticks are handy as support stakes for tall plants and vines. You can also use one as a hole digger.

If you have a dog, the stick could become a portable dog tender, but be kind. Use a broomstick as a hiking stick. Children can use them as bats for "stickball" games. Other uses include: flag poles for the side of the house, paint mixers, exercise sticks, and an aid in lifting things from dye solutions or hot water. How about an emergency cane if you sprain an ankle? (Heaven forbid.)

CARE OF YOUR CORN BROOM

If you give your broom good care it will serve you for a longer time. First, when you put it away in the closet do not stand it on the sweeping end. It will become bent and warped out of shape. It's best to hang it up after using. Water does not injure your broom—but dampen it, don't soak it. If it should get wet, shake it, then hang it up, sweeping end down. Don't stand it on end (either end) while wet. It will then serve you well.

During one of my trips to Illinois from California I purchased a broom at the Broomcorn Festival. Since I was carrying several packages the broom was a bit unwieldy. A member of the Arcola Chamber of Commerce offered to help.

ASSISTING VISITORS

The Chamber of Commerce of Arcola respects the lowly broom, and is always helpful in assisting visitors at the broomcorn festival in any way possible. They can give information regarding accommodations—motels and hotel available—if you would like to spend the night in order to take in more than one day of activities. Old-fashioned eateries in the area serve delicious country food. If time permits, a visit to the Rockome Gardens, west of Arcola, is truly a nostalgic trip. Also, many enjoy a tour of the Amish farm area.

Visitors who had to leave right after the festival remarked that the next time they came they would plan to stay longer. They were aware that in a short time apples would be ripe in the area, tree limbs heavy with delicious fruit. Persimmons, small but very sweet after a frost, would be ready to be picked. Foliage on many trees would be bright and beautiful with fall hues.

Mother, you would have enjoyed the festival. In concluding pages I have tried to include some of the things that you might have written had you been able to attend that famous celebration.

Broomcorn Nostalgia

CONCLUSION

We have attended the Broomcorn Festival as my mother wished, and after that I hope we have learned "all about broomcorn and brooms, and life in the olden days while broomcorn flourished."

While visiting in Arcola and attending the Festival, it became evident that its residents are loyal to the needs of their community. They appreciate the past and keep it alive. Their everyday lives are enriched by it. The distant past still stirs us. The past, not the future, tends to strengthen its hold upon us.

Through its annual Broomcorn Festival, Arcola, set down among the cornstalks of Central Illinois, is proof that residents are preserving a way of life Americans hold dear. Precious are their memories.

Field of Memories

People and happenings in the past tend to influence and mold us. My mother believed that **if we never lose sight of the past we are better able to look forward to the future.** Here are some interesting thoughts, reprinted from a trade publication, *The Automotive Booster*, during the presidency of Ronald Reagan. (Author unknown.)

> "You remember the real America if you can remember:
> When riots were unthinkable.
> When you left front doors open.
> When socialism was a dirty word.
> When the Flag was a sacred symbol.
> When criminals actually went to jail.
> When you weren't afraid to go out at night.
> When taxes were only a necessary nuisance...
> ...When clerks and repairmen tried to please you.
> When college kids swallowed goldfish, not acid.
> ...When you knew what the 4th of July stood for.
> When you never dreamed that our country could ever lose.
> When you bragged about your home town and home state.
> ...When people expected less, and valued what they had more.
> When politicians proclaimed their patriotism, and meant it.
> When everybody knew the difference between right and wrong.
> When things weren't perfect —but you never expected them to be.
> ...When you knew that the law would be enforced,

and your safety protected.
   ... When the law meant justice, and you felt a shiver of awe at the sight of a policeman.
   When you weren't embarrassed to say that this is the best country in the world.
   When America was a land filled with brave, proud, confident, hard-working people."

Regarding brooms, here is what the editor of *Broom and BroomCorn News* pointed out in an article in 1924, and it is still true today.

"The broom is old-fashioned and yet modern.
The broom we use today is not greatly unlike the first broom used. In principle and purpose it is practically the same.
Science has given civilization the electric lights, electric power, and many labor-saving devices, but the broom, **like the ancient device the wheel**, is one of the fundamental inventions that may be improved but never changed. At least one is found in most every home and business in every land, the old-fashioned broom to be used against an ancient enemy—dirt. It is still an indispensable household necessity, the most economical and dependable ally for cleanliness known to mankind. It is always ready to go, no electric wire is needed, ... no expensive repairs and upkeep. **The broom is here to stay.**"

The Broomcorn Festival is also here to stay. People want to partake of all that the original Broomcorn Palace of 1898 represents—the preservation of a way of life.

During her lifetime, my mother wore out many brooms. Not having one in her home was to her unthinkable. The day of the Broomcorn Festival, when she wanted to attend but could not, she picked up a broom and remarked, "I hope there will always be a broomcorn festival. I'm sure there will always be brooms."

The more things change, the more they remain the same. The corn broom continues to be a handy cleaning tool in most homes in America, as well as in other countries. Modernizing the home did not eliminate the broom.

Like a sunset leaving a happy glow in the sky, each broomcorn festival leaves those who attended it with a feeling that in nature there is always hope. Emily Dickinson, New England poetess, speaks of the sunset as a "housewife in the evening west" who ". . . sweeps with many colored brooms, and leaves the shreds behind . . ."

In recalling my mother and her butcher-knife hoeing, and my father's ploughing of fields for corn and hay, brings to mind a quotation from Eric Sloane's *America*:

> ". . . as long as man farms, which is as long as the world eats, there will still be the smell of hay and the sounds of farm life and with them a great respect for the farmer of the past who was poor, equipment-wise, but so rich in having lived the American life to its

fullest . . . Those who would find the spirit of early America must look first in the country."

Broomcorn, though scarce, is a crop that will never die. Like a precious antique, it is very valuable. Even if some day there might never be another acre planted, **broomcorn nostalgia** will still be present. Stories will be handed down to live on in generation after generation.

Field of Memories

GLOSSARY

Awned — bearded
Boot — the sheaf
Bract — modified leaf growing on a stalk
Broom Corn — the brush or head which is used in the manufacture of brooms and brushes
Brush — the seed heads of broom corn
Crooks — brush in which the fiber makes a distinct bend of 30 degrees or more
Fiber — panicle branches extending outward from the knuckle
Glumes — husks
Handle — the stem
Hurl — the long, fine brush suitable for use on the outside of brooms
Knuckle — the node where the fibers branch from the stem
Length* — short brush (measures less than 14");
  — medium (14 to 17") ;
  — long (17 to 23"), or over length (23" or over)
*as determined by measurements of the fiber taken from the knuckle to the top
Panicle — head, spike, or spikelet
Self-working — broom corn which can be used for both inside and outside of brooms
Spikes — short heads with the branches coming out all along the main stem

Tabling — a method of bending tall stalks of broom corn over, at waist level, diagonally across from adjacent rows forming a table of crossed stalks with the panicles extending beyond adjacent rows, bringing the head within easy reach of the cutter

Tip — the place near the end of the brush where the fibers will even up to the best advantage in trimming

Underwork — broom corn not suitable for hurl

RESOURCES

Arcola Chamber of Commerce
The Arcola Record-Herald, Broomcorn Festival 1976-94, various issues
Broom & Broom Corn News, Arcola, Illinois, Sept. 1974, John and Mary File
Dr. H. Hadley, Agronomist, University of Illinois
Illinois Farm Bureau – FAMILY
Paul A. Lindenmeyer, Arcola, IL, "Early History of Broom and Broomcorn Industry," N.P. Late 1920's/Early 1930
The Los Angeles Times, Charles Hillinger, "Broom Industry may be Facing Sweeping Change," 17 Sept. 1988, Business Pt. 4, P. 1
The Martins of Rockome, Arthur Martin, "The Story of Broomcorn," Rockome Pub. Foundation, N.D.
MEXICO Chamber of Commerce, Dept. of Public Relations
The Miami Herald, Dave Barry
The Thomas Monahan Company, Arcola, Illinois
Elizabeth Taft Murphy, *I Remember, Do you?* 1923 Milwaukee Ideals
National Broom & Mop Council, Chicago
Oklahoma State Univ., Agronomy Dept., Prof. D. E. Weibel, Broomcorn Lit./Photos 1978
Cynthia Rothrock, *The Early History of Arcola*, N.D.

Thomas J. Schlereth, *Victorian America.*, New York, Harper Collins, 1991

Eric Sloane's, *AMERICA*, New York, Galahad Books, 1982

The Texas A & M Univ. System – Broomcorn Production Progress Report No. 1468, 1952

U. S. Dept. of Agriculture –Farmers Bulletin No. 1631, 1930

D. E. Weibel, *Sorghum Production & Utilization*, Avi Pub., rpt 1965, Ch. 12

Field of Memories

CREDIT FOR ILLUSTRATIONS

Arcola Record-Herald, Arcola, Illinois
Dave Barry, *The Miami Herald*
John and Mary File, Champaign, Illinois
The Gazette Company, Cedar Rapids, Iowa
Lydia Hemrich, Effingham, Illinois
Burl Ives, Anacortes, Washington
Michelle Jaeger, Fresno, California
Mark Jones, Arthur, Illinois
Gertrud Lawson, San Diego
Mission Country, Goleta, California
R. K. O'Daniell, Champaign-Urbana *News Gazette*
Oklahoma State University, Agronomy Department
Mr. and Mrs. Norman Schanz, West Amana, Iowa
The Tintype Shoppes Photography, Arthur, Illinois
U.S. Department of Agriculture, Farmers Bulletin 1631
Don and Marie Ward, Newton, Illinois

Field of Memories

ABOUT THE AUTHOR

The author, Alice, was one of eight children in the Babbs family. She grew up on a farm in Southern Illinois during the depression years. Memories of her family life are woven through her book. She graduated from Lockyear's business college in Evansville, Indiana, and began secretarial work.

After her marriage to Herbert Smith, they raised two children, Madelyn "Maggie" and Edwin. Eventually, Mrs. Smith went back to secretarial work in the Midwest and later in California.

Now widowed, the author spends time in writing. She has had numerous articles and poems published. It was one of her bosses, "Pete" Dangermond, former Director of Parks and Recreation for the State of California, who encouraged her writing efforts.

Alice's hobbies include gardening, walking, and reading—especially mysteries, humor, and poetry. She also enjoys spending time with her children, grandchildren, great grandchildren, and step-family. She agrees with whoever wrote, "Itching for what you want doesn't do much good. **You've got to scratch for it.**" She believes that with faith and a sense of humor you can survive anything.

ORDER FORM

Please send _____ book(s) of *Broomcorn Nostalgia: Field of Memories* @ $12.95 each (USA) softbound edition to:

Name: _____

Address: _____

City: _____ State: _____ Zip _____

Shipping & Handling @ $3.95 ea _____

Book(s) @ $12.95 ea _____

Sub-total _____

CA residents add Sales Tax **1.00**

TOTAL enclosed (Check or Money Order) _____

SEND ORDER TO:

Olde Mill Publishing
P.O. Box 6342
Santa Barbara, CA 93160

ORDER FORM

Please send _____ book(s) of *Broomcorn Nostalgia: Field of Memories* @ $12.95 each (USA) softbound edition to:

Name: _____

Address: _____

City: _____ State: _____ Zip _____

Shipping & Handling @ $3.95 ea _____

Book(s) @ $12.95 ea _____

Sub-total _____

CA residents add Sales Tax **1.00**

TOTAL enclosed (Check or Money Order) _____

SEND ORDER TO:

Olde Mill Publishing
P.O. Box 6342
Santa Barbara, CA 93160